DECORATING IDEAS

New room-by-room decorating tips

By the Editors of
Better Homes & Gardens

© MEREDITH PUBLISHING COMPANY, 1960. ALL RIGHTS RESERVED
PRINTED IN THE UNITED STATES OF AMERICA

Contents

Chapter 1 What goes with what 4

Chapter 2 How to use color 12

Chapter 3 Window treatments 34

Chapter 4 Furniture arrangement 52

Decorating ideas for

Chapter 5 Living rooms 62

Chapter 6 Dining rooms 80

Chapter 7 Kitchens 90

Chapter 8 Family rooms 100

Chapter 9 Children's rooms 110

Chapter 10 Bedrooms 120

Chapter 11 Bathrooms 130

Chapter 12 Dens, guest rooms and studies 140

Chapter 13 Halls and stairways 150

Credits and acknowledgments on page 160

Introduction

If you prize beauty and good design in the furnishings of your home, we believe you will find this book rewarding. Its goal is to awaken and advance your own taste, develop your ability to discriminate, increase your confidence in the choices you make.

Whether you prefer Traditional or Contemporary styles in home furnishings, this book can help you with your decorating problems. Nor is it directed to any one budget level. Basic good taste has little to do with price tags. Rather, it is the faculty of recognizing differences between honest and shoddy design, harmonious and inharmonious color combinations, appropriate and inappropriate groupings of elements in a decorating scheme.

This is a browsing book. It gives you practical, down-to-earth information on how to choose and use color, how to arrange furniture, how to select window treatments. It gives you tested and proven suggestions on the art of buymanship, advises you on how to shop wisely for the materials you need.

We are indebted to Jo Bull for her able assistance in developing and writing this book. Mrs. Bull has worked with us for many years and has had years of experience in interpreting, observing, reporting on styles, materials, trends. The book meets all decorating problems with realism and practicality, seeing each one as a challenge which can be turned to decorating advantage.

We also gratefully acknowledge our debt to the skilled decorators and designers whose work we show; to the photographers and artists who have captured the effects they sought and created.

The Editors
Better Homes & Gardens

Chapter one

What goes with what

You want a pretty, comfortable home that reflects your tastes. When faced with "What Goes With What," consider suitability. You wouldn't wear a lace-trimmed satin blouse with a tweed suit skirt. You *would* wear it with silks and velvets. The same principle applies to home furnishings. Other tips to help you choose:

1. If you like a Traditional look, and there aren't enough family heirlooms to go around, choose your period, use reproductions and adaptations. Take advantage of the professional help which a store's home-planning experts can give you.

2. You can get opulent effects with comparatively inexpensive materials: plastic brick or stone-patterned wall coverings; terrazzo or marble-grained vinyl floors; Traditional-patterned curtain and drapery fabrics that drip-dry; light fixtures with lacquer finishes that never need polishing; man-made fibers in carpets and rugs that laugh at spills and spots; wool carpets that are mothproofed for a lifetime.

3. When you shop for either color or style, don't try for exact matches—blend to get the effect.

4. Look for modern comfort and materials: tables with imperturbable tops; cushions filled with fluffy, spring-back man-made fibers; fabrics that repel dust, spots; Traditional-styled lamps with today's height.

Mix periods and styles to achieve an individual, just-for-you look

The "rule" is to combine informal things *or* formal, not both. The handcrafted look of modern pottery "goes" with Early American; fine formal Contemporary crystal blends with elegant Empire. Set theme with one style, add others as accents.

...in casual Modern

There's a new carefree way of life . . . a real sit-on-the-floor, shoes-off sort of feeling. The danger in decorating to this new freedom is that it can be so casual as to be haphazard. But if you keep it simple, serene, with a minimum of clutter, you'll find it warm and friendly, and most easy to keep. When you shop for casual Modern, keep in mind that:

1. The contrast of textures is the main ingredient of simple Modern. Play smooth surfaces against rough, as in highly polished paneling next to rough brick, satiny fabrics against mat-finish paint.

2. Natural materials, or copies of them are in vogue. Grass cloth, or paper printed to look like it; rough brick, or three-dimensional plastic brick wall covering; wooden floors, or wood-grained vinyl; wood paneling that comes pre-finished, or wallpaper that resembles it; hand-woven fabrics, or materials that simulate these textures . . . all these are marks of distinguished Contemporary decorating.

3. Accent pieces have a hand-crafted look, are often peasant art imported from other countries.

4. Colors are simple, usually blending rather than contrasting, with brilliance reserved for accents. Among the most popular combinations are blue and green, and the classic Scandinavian folk colors of blue, red, and yellow.

5. Window treatments are simple, with top preference going to hand-woven blinds (or copies), and to draw-draperies, alone or with shades or curtains.

6. Wood finishes are natural, not too highly polished, with the grain showing. You'll find many tables, benches and chests with no-scar, easy-care plastic tops in almost any color or finish.

7. Fabrics simulate hand-woven materials, or are patterned with geometric designs or stripes.

8. Hanging light fixtures of simple Modern design in pottery, glass or metal are widely used.

9. Wall-to-wall carpeting in muted tones is popular. Accent and area rugs show beauty of wood or hard-surfaced colored, patterned floors.

...in Early American

Early American, or Colonial, began with the Pilgrims, continued with other early settlers such as the Pennsylvania Dutch. Because ship space was at a premium, the average man could bring little in the way of furnishings or tools with him.

Early American designs were mostly handmade from native woods — rough copies of styles prevalent at home. Their casual charm, nostalgic reference to our beginnings, make them most popular today. When you shop, consider these style points:

1. Early lamps burned oil. Today's adaptations take their shapes from these lamps or jars of the period. Shades are often of homespun-type fabrics.

2. Shutters were common, sometimes dressed up with short curtains of crudely spun material, or of stylized and geometric prints, looking like woodcuts.

3. Dyes were largely vegetable, colors usually rich brown, strong red, muted green, butternut yellow.

4. Every scrap of fabric was saved and reworked. Patchwork prints, available now, are suitable.

5. Wall coverings were originally fabric rather than paper, so typical designs are borrowed from old trunk linings or pillow tickings, and are stylized.

6. Pressed glass was available, often decorated with fruits and flowers. Amethyst, cranberry, amber colors were prized. Today's copies even preserve the seams of the original molds.

7. Wall shelves often took the place of closets or more formal storage pieces. Today they hold copies of pewter porringers and pitchers, and stainless steel adaptations of early hollow ware.

8. Rag rugs, or adaptations, are authentic.

9. Real or reproduced, old tools, such as cranberry picker or dough tray are interesting accompaniments.

...in formal Contemporary

← Formal furnishings denote an orderliness of habit... a "sit down and be served" kind of living and entertaining. They show an appreciation of beauty, of true art in both form and design. Contemporary formality is characterized by elegant materials coupled with simplicity of line, and by intricately wrought, fine accessories. Look for:

1. Tables and chests that hug the floor... some storage pieces look like architectural built-ins, soar to the ceiling. High or low, they are designed to give a measure of individuality to modern boxy rooms, are seldom of medium height.

2. Light fixtures are often used instead of table lamps, give greater flexibility for arrangement.

3. Window treatments are simple, architectural... such as draw-draperies, pull-up shades, screens or fabric panels that reflect architectural designs, derive from shojis or geometric forms.

4. Textures are smooth, fabrics are rich and elegant. Colors are subtly related combinations, or strong contrasts of brilliant tones.

5. Accent pieces are often Oriental; formal English and French antiques or reproductions are also used as appropriate companions to formal Contemporary.

6. Flooring is smooth, frequently of modern design in vinyl or linoleum. Wall-to-wall carpeting in brilliant colors is popular, as are boldly patterned rugs.

...in French Provincial

In the last days of the French monarchy, just before the Revolution, there was a vogue for being "natural," with elegant designs that were simplified versions of court designs. Its graceful lines, mellow woods, soft colors, make Provincial one of our most popular period styles. Other characteristics to look for if you're decorating in this style:

1. Decorative pieces took their forms directly from nature—delicate flower-forms or patterned vases, animal and bird figures.

2. Rich fabrics, such as velvets, tapestries, brocades, were typical. You can buy these today in synthetic fabrics, easy to care for and spot-resistant.

3. Most popular colors were muted pastels—green, blue, rose, with lots of white.

4. Fruit woods were used for furniture—pear, cherry, walnut. A great deal of today's Provincial furniture is walnut with a soft amber finish, often distressed, which means it has simulated wear markings.

5. Many individual pieces of furniture were painted in white or pastels, with floral decorations. See the handsome painted furniture on the market today.

6. Fabrics were often in toile patterns, first made in France, characterized by one-color printing, often of a pastoral scene, or with classical or Chinese motifs. Other popular patterns were plaids, stripes, fruit and flower prints, or quilted designs.

7. Wallpaper was first made in France, with flocked or floral patterns typically Provincial.

8. Lace curtains were a must. They are available today in no-stretch, no-iron fibers.

9. Wood floors were costly, so scraps were saved, pieced together into parquet. It's available today in prefinished squares, lays like tile.

10. Wall decorations, such as sconces, were ornate, often fashioned of wrought metal, delicately painted to resemble real fruit or flowers.

...in 18th Century

← Also called Williamsburg or Federal, these are the formal furnishings of Revolutionary times. They reflect the worldly knowledge of men of taste and education, with contacts in both the Orient and Europe. You'll find:

1. Hardwoods were plentiful so wood floors were popular. Choose from today's varieties of wood floors, or wood-patterned vinyls.

2. Wing chairs were favorites, were practical for shutting off drafts.

3. Paul Revere designed coffee services and bowls in both pewter and silver. Authentic copies of Revere designs are available today.

4. Popular colors were green, white, brown, and the blue we call "Williamsburg."

5. Venetian blinds covered Colonial windows, inspired by the jalousies our young navy found in Mediterranean countries.

6. Oriental rugs were cherished, as were the blue and white Oriental designs of accent pieces and tableware brought by clipper ship.

7. Both wallpapers and fabrics featured patterns that pictured historic events or flowers. Florals were often light, on a dark ground. Handblocked prints were prized.

8. Eagles as a symbol of American independence became a popular motif.

9. Glass shields to keep candles from flickering have inspired today's hurricane lamps. Brass, often ornamented, was popular.

...in Empire

The Classic or Empire style originated in Napoleonic France. It was inspired by the interest in classical antiquities of Rome, Greece and Egypt resulting from French conquests. The "Contemporary" of its day, its crispness indicates a revolt from the ornate designs of the preceding period. When you shop for Empire for your home, remember these points:

1. Marble floors typify the Classic mood. Yours might be a roto-printed vinyl floor covering as shown here.

2. Classic chair styles were adapted from ancient Roman designs. Popular black finish can be found today.

3. Urns and columns are basic Empire designs. You'll find them in plant stands, pedestal bases, lamp shafts.

4. Pictures of historic ruins or of Napoleonic battle scenes are appropriate.

...in Victorian

The Victorians admired opulence, liked ornamentation. Cranberry red was a favorite color, patterns and designs exploited the facilities of the new mass-production machines.

Today's adaptations are restrained, but still capture the warmth of the period. For a Gay Nineties' flavor in your home, consider these points:

1. Pressed glass was—and still is—popular, sometimes with several colors in combination. Milk glass in fancy shapes also "belongs."

2. Floral patterns were everywhere, from china to tapestries, with roses a favorite. Tapestries often had black backgrounds. Similar designs are available today in easy-care man-made fibers.

3. Typical period fabrics included needle-point designs, velvets, floral chintzes, white-on-white motifs. Today needle-point designs are printed on cotton, velvets are spot- and crush-resistant, draperies in the Victorian mood come ready-made.

4. Glass domes covered everything imaginable, are practical dust-protectors for ornate decorations.

5. Carved and ornamented chairs with matching settee were in vogue. Today's designs are simpler.

6. Gaslight shed a soft but inadequate glow. Electrified adaptations give better light. Both table lamps and fixtures are available in period styles.

7. Cranberry red was popular for wallpaper, often flocked. You can buy paper with a flocked pattern, or real flocking that's washable. Other popular patterns were lavish, characterized by curving lines, pierced shellwork, or lush floral designs.

8. Most Victorian windows were topped with swags, often damask with tasseled trim. Austrian shades, popular then, can be purchased ready-made in synthetics, or made at home with a kit that contains all the necessary cords, tapes, instructions.

9. Marble-topped tables and chests were fashionable, used much carved ornamentation. Most of today's are finished in dark, reddish mahogany.

10. Rose-strewn carpets were the height of fashion. Be cautious in copying if your room is small.

← **5.** Bold stripes were favorites. Used here for draperies, they're equally effective as upholstery. Fleur-de-lis window shade is several lengths of polished cotton sewed together.

6. Preferred wallpaper and drapery patterns used subtle colors. Tone-on-tone damask patterns with Classical motifs are authentic.

7. Upholstery fabrics featured a silky look, medallion patterns.

8. Classic colors included white, gold, black and a sharp, deep green we call Empire, because it was Napoleon's favorite shade.

9. Decorative pieces were often copies of classical antiques, or ornamented with Napoleonic "N" or a stylized honeybee design.

Chapter two

How to use color

Start your color plan with colors you like; adapt to your home with these 9 rules

Color works magic. Use it with a lavish hand, remembering the following simple principles as you plan the effect you want:

1. Bold colors advance, pale colors recede, can make a room look smaller or bigger.

2. Contrasting colors emphasize each other; closely blended colors conceal defects.

3. One bold pattern is usually enough . . . use it dramatically. Don't detract from it with another eye-catching design.

4. Warmth and excitement are suggested by the colors of fire . . . red, yellow, orange. Coolness and peace come with blues and greens and white which are borrowed from nature's palette.

5. Unequal areas of color are more pleasing . . . use a major tone to cover about two-thirds of a room, vary with accents.

6. Color is affected by its neighbors. Test colors against each other before you buy.

7. Wood surfaces have color, too. Consider table tops and chair frames in your scheme.

8. Large areas of color look deeper, so be cautious when you select wall tones.

9. The final effect of the plan should include "something dark, something light, something dull, and something bright."

Cool and calm, this white and blue scheme conveys the restfulness of sky and clouds, is saved from monotony by tiny flashes of bright accent.

Space-expanding white is used on five-sixths of the room's area—on walls and ceiling. Its appeal is strengthened by the contrasting blue. A white blind, running from floor to ceiling, and blending into the wall, softens the architectural break of the window; it blends, too, with the geometrical design of the chimney breast.

Remember the little poem in rule 9 across the page? "Something dark" is accent of end table, fireplace, fire tools. "Something light" is walls, coffee table. "Something dull is the texture of carpet and upholstery. "Something bright" is paint surfaces, highly glazed birds, bowl.

Neighboring hues are good partners

An easy color scheme to carry out combines colors next to each other on a color wheel—neighboring hues which are so close they could be called "kissing cousins."

Because of their kinship, they will look well together. Choose one color for major areas; use it in enough strength to make your point. Add smaller quantities of one or more "cousins" to complete the scheme.

...Start with blue

← *In this scheme, the colors range from blue-violet to bright green*

Blue is the basic color here, massed on the painted walls, in chair upholstery, divider panel, lamp shade, decorative touches.

"Cousin" blue-violet was chosen for the area rug under the dining table, repeated in a glass jar in the foreground. Kin-colors on the other side of blue—blue-green and green—were added in the ottoman, divider and glass bottle.

Colors here range from blue to red

The blue of the wallpaper set the color theme here, repeated in dado and window frame, strengthened in the tablecloth. "Cousins" violet, rose-red and rose-pink appear in the carpet, china, napkins and chair seats.

Fashion note is painted furniture used to add freshness, and to echo the neutral white found in the pattern of the wallpaper.

...start with *gold*

← *Yellow-green scheme relates two rooms*

Kin colors of golden yellow and yellow-green are repeated in two areas. Yellow is the dominant note in the study area, in walls, glowing lamp shade.

Green is emphasized on bedroom walls, yellow in the spread. Both areas use a soft green wall-to-wall carpeting which unites rooms visually. Accents of gleaming brass are effective in both rooms.

Ivory-yellow ranges to deep red-orange

Those warm, inviting "cousins," yellow and orange, make this family-guest room friendly in appearance.

Largest areas of wall and floor are soft ivory-yellow and dull terra-cotta red. In a higher key are the wall of orange, chair, spread and basket in redder hues. See-through divider combines all of the colors used in the rest of the scheme.

Choose the color combination *you* like

The happiest rooms to visit and to live in are those whose color schemes mirror personal taste—not merely a current vogue for a high-style hue.

One way to decide on the major decorating color you'll like to live with is to analyze your wardrobe. Do the soft or neutral shades predominate, with the more vivid hues used largely for costume accessories or for clothing that you wear only occasionally?

If so, the chances are you'll be happiest in a room which follows this same general pattern of color distribution—a quiet shell with bright accents.

But if you wear vivid colors well and often, you are a person who is temperamentally suited to enjoy a room that displays vibrant hues generously.

Shades of green freshened with white provide a restful background for living

Tones and tints of yellow-green are given variety through textures ranging from tweedy to smooth. To obtain contrast, masses of white are used in window treatment and in chair upholstery. Such light colors can be practical, too, if you use newer fabrics treated to resist soil and stains.

Color scheme designed for those who like to live with warmer hues

Blue and orange, opposites on the color wheel, are the basic colors for this attractive room. A warm tint of orange chosen for the walls offers contrast to the blue of upholstery fabric, draperies, and decorative accents. Dark finish of furniture emphasizes and repeats color of dramatic crossbeams.

Consider these major areas of color

1 Background is first—big areas call for softer tones

A brilliant plaid, to be used as an accent, was the basis for the scheme in this room. Its colors range from beige to gold, to plum, purple, shades of blue and green.

The lavender tones appealed to the family. Because color is more intense in large quantities, a warm, soft tone was selected for the walls, a lighter tint for the ceiling. The color has the property of receding under bright light, seems gayer on a dismal day.

A shade of neutral beige in carpet and draperies stems from one of the colors in plaid.

Secret of satisfactory color combinations is to blend, not try for an exact match.

2 You can afford stronger colors for major pieces

Even though sofas and chairs may seem big, their total bulk is considerably less than that of walls and floors. Here you can pleasantly use stronger, deeper colors if you wish.

The old furniture in this room was co-ordinated by using the same fabric on chair, sofa and hassock, in a bluish-plum shade that blends with purples and blues of the plaid.

Wood has color, too. For a lighter look, most pieces were chosen in beige tones that go with carpet and draperies. The big coffee table reflects the deep tone of the fireplace.

3 *Bright accent colors give a room individuality, make it sparkle*

The plaid is most prominently used in the screen separating the living and dining areas. It is picked up and distributed in a bench pad and a pillow on the sofa. A smaller brilliant note is struck by bluish-red in the pull-up chair and a sofa cushion, strengthening and brightening the basic purple.

Watch for color combinations you like ...adapt them to your own home

The way colors are distributed is a key to adapting scheme to your home

There are three major color areas in this room. First is a mass of olive green in the bedspreads; second, a large area of turquoise in the carpet; third, bright accents of purple in the chairs. This room is high-styled, but its elegant color scheme will work as well in a more budget-minded home.

Everywhere you go . . . to a friend's home, to a hotel or motel, to a store's model rooms . . . you'll find color used imaginatively. Your favorite magazine prints hundreds of pictures a year, showing the expert color techniques of professional decorators. You will not want—or need—to copy these rooms exactly. Study them to see the proportions in which the various colors are used . . . then adapt these proportions to your own home. The result will be a fresh scheme, suited to your way of living.

Try same colors in living room

Here the colors fall in the same proportion, with olive green massed on sofa and ceiling-high draperies. A marble patterned wallpaper takes the place of the stone wall.

Good color scheme knows no "period"

Colors are equally handsome in a Traditional room. Smooth-surfaced flooring is in the original greenish-blue; heavily textured wall covering substitutes effectively for the stone.

Color can affect the way you feel

Combinations of colors and textures with which you surround yourself have a real effect on the way you feel, the way you live. Bright tones, dramatically combined, give a sense of gaiety... rich colors, smooth textures, have an elegant air. By and large, the cool colors are soothing, the warm tones are more exciting.

In any room that is mostly devoted to sitting or reading, or quiet family evenings, you'll probably like neutral or cool tones, sparked with just enough bright color to banish dullness. Or you can wake up a room to party brilliance, with a combination of vivid, warm, friendly colors.

Warm earth tones and sleek textures combine to achieve inviting elegance

Rich colors and fabrics have a friendly and inviting air. The luxurious sweep of autumn-toned carpet underscores the more fragile look of white walls, draperies and sofa covering, blends well with wood finishes. A wise combination of hanging fixture and lamps will make this room glow after sundown as well.

Cool colors, light woods give this variation delicate formality

Blue and green, the tones of repose and tranquility, bring dignity even to informal styles. Floor and walls are the same cool color, broken only by the neutral, blending colors of wood finishes and drapery. A few dark pieces furnish the needed contrast.

Strong colors, bright accents and sturdy textures cast a gay spell

The formula is a bright mass of yellow in sofa and ceiling; strong primary accents; a quiet shell of white. The furniture arrangement is a bonus—cozy sofa grouping for a few people, easily moved snack tables with pull-up bench and pillows for parties.

You can change a mood with color

Do you feel drab and moody at the end of a day ... or too keyed up to rest and relax? The medicine you need might be a change of color scheme, to pep you up, calm you down. For an easy formula, try the "kissing cousins," or related colors.

Big masses of peaceful blues are warmed with violet and rose accents

Always use enough of your basic color to set the proper mood. Here, soft blues give a feeling of serenity, an aura of perfect relaxation. The brighter related tones of violet and rose combine to chase monotony. Furniture arrangement note: Set furniture *on* a rug, not half on, half off.

Spring greens give a feeling of space

If your husband is crowded into a tiny, glare-filled office during the day, he undoubtedly wants to feel in his home a sense of space; he wants to be the lord of the manor. Here, a pale shell of young green, with added touches of sky-blue, refreshes eye and heart.

Pep up with a warm and happy color

Lift the spirit with a combination of vivid colors against a sweep of neutral tone. Here a mass of yellow is made more brilliant by a touch of its cousin, orange. The delicately flowing movement of a branch softens the square lines of Contemporary furniture.

Matching pattern of draperies and sofa placed next each other makes room look lopsided →

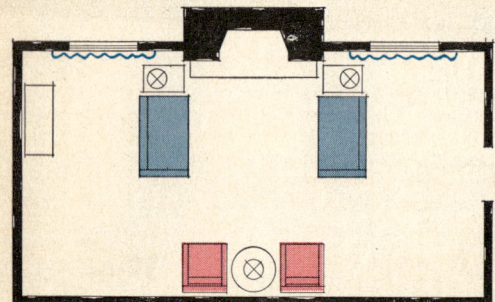

WEAK

Despite a basically pleasing color scheme — the room shell in a warm, neutral beige, with contrast in patterned fabric as well as in bright red solid color — this room looks drab.

Why? Because placement of colors is inept. The drapery pattern which runs almost from floor to ceiling, with the same pattern used for sofas placed close to windows, makes this side of the room too light to balance the visually heavier red of the chairs which are opposite.

Balance is the pleasing effect you get when the shapes and colors in a room are well distributed. As you plan a color scheme, imagine the room as a box, with a center point in the middle, halfway from side to side, halfway from top to bottom.

Formal balance results if all the objects and colors on one side of the imaginary point are repeated in exactly equal amounts on the other.

Informal balance results when unlike amounts of color are used on each side of the center point, and at different distances from each other, in a way that pleases the eye, seems well distributed.

On a teeter-totter, a heavy weight close to the center can be balanced by a light weight further away. So with color. A mass of bright color near the center of a room can be balanced by a smaller amount of the same hue at its outer edges.

Vertical color balance should be considered, too. Color placed at the same height all around a room is dull. For variety, place some high, some low.

Color balance is important

←

Patterns across the room from each other, reds repeated, result in a harmonious room

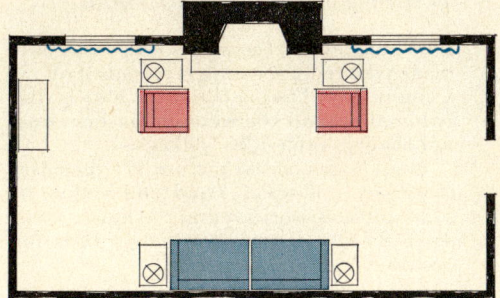

STRONG

Color is balanced, both vertically and horizontally. Blue and white pattern of the floor length draperies is repeated in the bulk of low sofa across the room.

Bright red chairs separate the two masses of pattern, with reds reappearing in sofa pillows, in bowl of fruit on wall chest.

And there's a better traffic pattern than in floor plan opposite. People can walk into the room without swerving around sofa ends.

The most appealing color scheme is greatly handicapped if colors aren't effectively distributed in a room. In placing color to achieve balance, think in terms of three areas: walls and floors, large furniture, decorative accents.

A rough floor plan, with furniture sketched in and colored is very helpful in the planning stage. If all major color is located on one side of the room, the result will be poor color balance.

Redistribute color, placing some on opposite sides until you get a balanced arrangement. This experiment may indicate a switch of colors on some pieces of furniture, or rearrangement.

Any color that's basic to your decorating scheme should make more than a solo appearance. It should recur in several parts of the room. You might use color from a drapery pattern for pillows on a sofa across the room, for lamp bases or shades, for ash trays or other accents such as picture mats or frames, or in a bowl of fruit or flowers.

Shift color emphasis for a new look

Cool blue walls blend with a color in the picture, give an airy look to a bright and sunny room

Pale blue pushes the major wall areas out, makes the room seem bigger, cools it off on a sunny day. Deeper, brighter blue is distributed around the room in leather chair upholstery, table tiles, pillows.

Beige tones of the picture are repeated in carpet and wood. Gold and yellow in sofas and accessories warm the blues. Twin sofas serve as convenient single beds for occasional overnight guests.

Beige tones shift to walls, give a warm and welcoming look

Same color scheme, different distribution, brings an entirely new look. Here, warm beige and brown taken from the picture blend wall, sofas, and furniture finish. Blue, yellow, gold are bright accents.

Sharp contrasts of color value make this room striking and dramatic

Bold, brilliant red dramatizes the good proportions of the fireplace wall. The mass of white in pictures and frames repeats the molding color, emphasizes the sweep of the chimney breast, repeats wall and upholstery color.

Blending values of the same colors reflect a softer, homier mood

Any color scheme that appeals to you can be translated into your own surroundings. For a dramatic look, choose color values that contrast. For a friendly, soft look, choose values that blend into each other.

Here, red is softened to pink, used on all the walls. Pink and white striped upholstery fabric blends together the walls, drapery pattern color, paint trim and white carpet. Light fabrics and carpets such as these are practical with today's soil and stain repellent finishes.

Let color flow from room to room

Consider your whole house when you plan a color scheme. A good basic plan can be varied to give an individual look to each room, yet maintain continuity.

You can even camouflage some colors you think difficult. For example, if you have a pink built-in kitchen but want a scheme of turquoise and bittersweet, choose a patterned fabric containing all three colors; use it for curtains, place mats, accents. Pink will blend into over-all plan.

Employ color continuity

The dining room is separated from the living room only by a fireplace divider, so a related look was obtained by using identical rug color.

At the same time, room achieves separateness through the use of green paint on its walls.

Start your planning with living room colors

Wide expanse of white brick fireplace and picture windows dictated a choice of warm colors. Green carpet reflects out-of-doors, is warmed by yellow and orange.

The kitchen features yellow

Yellow and green flow into the kitchen, with yellow becoming dominant, green secondary, and the orange accent notes repeated.

Paneled storage cabinet brings in wood tones found in living area.

Wood tones form subtle background for the family room color scheme

Soft browns, picked up from the wood tones of living area, dominate the family room. The yellow appears in the soffit and window framing, green in chairs, door, and wall storage panel. Substituting for the mass of white of living room fireplace is the Mondrian-like wall treatment employed in this room.

Accent orange becomes dominant in the bedroom

Adjoining bed and bath are well related. Since bathroom tile was blue, bedroom walls were painted a similar tone, the chair covered in blue and white fabric. Orange, living room accent, was made dominant in bedspread color and furniture finish.

Bath blends with bedroom

Blue tile is enlivened by orange and white towels. Plus value here is a plastic panel concealing the overhead fluorescent tube lighting.

Chapter three

Decorating ideas for windows

Windows serve three functional purposes: they let in light, provide for circulation of air, give you a view.

The fourth purpose is beauty—the way in which you drape or curtain them to make your home more attractive.

Use the following tips to make work easier, get most effective window treatment:
1. Avoid snags by covering end of curtain rod with transparent tape before threading.
2. For good looks, curtains should be two to three times wider than total width of area to be covered. The more filmy the fabric, the more fullness you will need.
3. Shorten curtains from the top . . . it's best not to tamper with a neat hem.
4. In measuring for full-length draperies, allow for thickness of rug and pad.
5. Hang ready-made draperies on traverse rods as professionals do, with the last two hooks in center as master carriers.
6. Get a professional look in draperies by creasing them properly. Run your hand up and down, gently creasing fold between your fingers. Tie them loosely with strips of fabric. Leave them tied for a few days until the crease has become set.

Take accurate measurements before you shop . . . have them with you when you buy

← There are three "correct" curtain or drapery lengths . . . to the sill, to the apron, to about a quarter inch above floor. This third measurement gives a full-length look but prevents draperies from dragging.

For informal curtains that are to cover only the glass area, measure the window width as shown by the short arrow in picture.

Measure every window in → the room, even if they look the same. There may be slight variations in size that need to be considered.

Ready-made curtains are labeled in inches, so take measurements that way.

↑ Curtains look better if they are gathered to cover rod around the curve to meet wall or woodwork.

For the proper fullness, add about 6 inches to the measurement you've already taken, in order to cover projection of about 3 inches at either end of rod.

A modern version of cutwork draperies covers both window wall and shutters

Contemporary felt drapery fabric unites antique furnishings from Pennsylvania and Mexican treasures. In the bay, design gives both privacy and light pattern. At short windows, it is tacked over wood shutters, finished with white molding.

Brighten adjoining rooms with harmonizing styles

When you can look from one room into another and see the windows of both, treatments should be in harmony, but not necessarily identical.

At one window you may want to shut out an ugly view; at another, let in lots of sunshine but reduce glare; at still another open up to a pretty garden and circulate fresh air.

If each window problem is different, each treatment should be planned accordingly. One answer might be to use two different fabrics—one plain, one patterned—which have a common dominant color that visually relates the two.

Another solution could be the use of the same kind of valance at all windows, even though the rest of the window treatments aren't the same.

Window treatment for a sunroom harmonizes with that of adjoining bedroom

Venetian blinds plus cafe curtains form a functional treatment for the windows of a sunroom opening off a bed-sitting room.

Ruffle of print material serves both to unify the group of windows and disguise the brackets supporting bookshelves above.

Pattern of fabric in ruffle also matches that of the wing chair's slip cover.

Venetian blinds in wall color rather than white establish a related look between these windows and those of bedroom— pictured on the facing page — which are draped with fabric of the same wall blue.

White cafes under blue draperies match the cafes used in the sunroom.

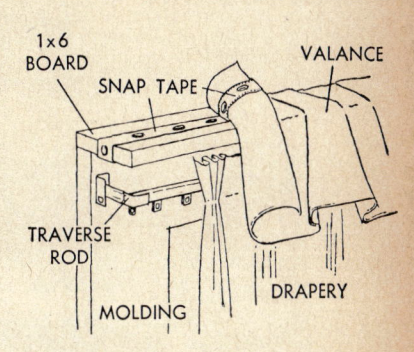

For a smooth, tailored appearance, try this method of attaching a valance.

Install a board over top of window molding, support with angle irons, and equip with strip of snap tape tacked in place.

Matching snap tape on the valance makes an easy task of removing it for cleaning or laundry.

For extra flair, valance is stiffened with a lining made of buckram.

Bedroom window treatment controls light and privacy

To give an unbroken line, the bedroom window is covered with a full-length drapery and valance blending in color with walls. This shuts out the light and gives nighttime privacy, too. Soft valance echoes the line of drapery folds.

Dainty cafes under the draperies

When this room is used as a daytime study or sitting room, light's controlled, view possible with the translucent curtains matching those in sunroom. Decorating note: pictures hung at left are placed to balance chair at right.

You can make these easy-to-iron curtains with ordinary straight hems. Sew on rings at evenly spaced intervals. To adjust, push down between rings with finger until folds are even.

Bright cornice adds cheer and color

The vivid line of cornice here adds a lovely look of length to the room. Warming the neutral tones of the rest of the scheme, the color is repeated in strength in the divider poles, cushions, and room accents.

Valances solve architectural problems

Full, long draperies, topped by around-the-corner valances, cover both windows and doors, disguising the various heights and sizes. One-way rods control them. Strong pattern is repeated in bed skirt and pillows.

New ways with valances and cornices

Popular once again are those finishing touches for windows—the decorative valances and cornices that add so much softness to a room.

There are some easy rules for using cornices or valances. First, don't let them overpower the rest of the window in size. Too deep, too heavy, they will give the impression of leaning into the room. Don't let them overpower in color or pattern. If you use bold pattern here, repeat it elsewhere in the room to give balance to the scheme.

While you're planning, consider the possibility of valance lighting. It will bring your evening lighting from the same direction as daytime sunshine, and will also supply good general illumination that enhances the room's furnishings.

Swag gives height to an ordinary window

The draped swag begins well above the top of the window frame, giving it size and importance. It also repeats the motif of the wallpaper dado. A Traditional theme is furthered by the solid wood panels around the frame, shutters that cover the opening.

Do you have a window that's too tall and narrow? Here are three ways to disguise it.

Top: Let your drapery fabric blend in color with the wall, cover the cornice with it, too. It will seem part of the background.

Center: Widen the looks of the window by draping the fabric back over knobs; use a plain cornice with a horizontal feeling.

Bottom: Hang the drapery material outside the window frame; use a deep valance.

Pick a pattern

By emphasizing your windows with draperies in a bold pattern, you can feature them as a major decorative element. To treat them as background, use identical patterns for walls, windows.

In either case, it is effective to repeat a pattern elsewhere in the room—in the chair coverings, pillows, other accents. If the sole use of pattern is at the windows, choose one of its prominent colors to appear elsewhere in the room in mass. Single, large use of pattern is apt to give the room a lopsided appearance.

Try repetition for importance

Make a small pattern important by using it for draperies, cornice, bedspreads, padded headboards. Choose colors from the pattern for upholstery, toss pillows, other accents.

To make a small room look larger, select a small pattern which will be in scale with the room's dimensions and furniture.

Frame a window with pattern

Treat a view window so it looks like a true entryway to the outdoors. Here, two sections of a three-section window are covered with shutters, the whole topped with a ruffled valance to match the wallpaper.

Shutter sections are hinged to open wide for added sunlight, close for a cozy feeling.

Define a dining area with bold pattern

The dining end of a multipurpose room is defined with a wall of traditionally patterned paper, matching fabric at the windows. The simple valance is hung at ceiling height to preserve continuity.

Draperies and valance cover entire wall of dining area, right up to the desk-divider. Corner window is uncovered by hardware that pulls fabric to right.

Try a circular cut

You can sometimes soften an angular look in a room with simple valances cut from a circle pattern. They can fall gently into folds, or be tacked or caught with rings.

Lined with buckram, they'll swell in permanent stiffness. Unlined, they'll fall into neat folds. For a gentler curve, use only part of a circle. For extra fullness, use a greater portion of a circle. You can hang these valances from rods, or snap them onto boards fastened over the window frame, as shown on page 37.

Classic swag effect comes from circle

A circular cut is the basis of this simple valance. Its effect of a series of small swags is achieved by catching points about a third of the way down from the top, tacking them to top hem, hanging with rings from a rod. Color of the band at the bottom of valance is picked up from wallpaper mural.

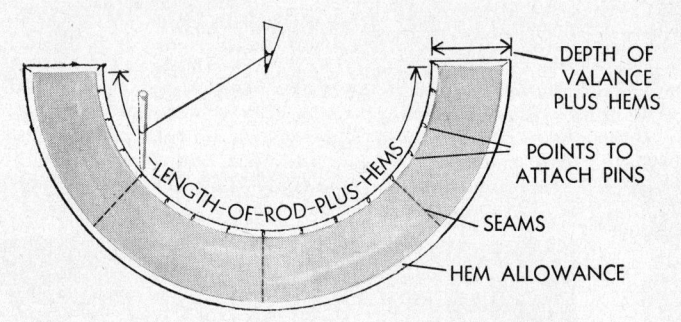

Inner curve of valance pattern is length of curtain rod plus hem allowance, fullness between rings. Draw pattern on newspaper, allow for hems.

Valance is cut like a circular skirt or jabot, using a half-circle of fabric with rings tacked on at 6- to 8-inch intervals. Cut lining same size, making sure both fabrics are pre-shrunk. Adjust rings for added fullness.

Deep valance adds height

Space between top of window and the window frame is completely filled with the soft folds of this circular-cut valance. Pattern carries bedspread motif across room. Draperies installed outside of frame add to wide look.

Shades are infinitely variable

There's been a revolution in window shades. The extension of choice beyond old-fashioned green, tan or white lets you use shades as a basic part of a decorating scheme—not just for light control.

You can have them custom made to match wall color, or in a bright accent hue. Or you can use your own fabric, fastening it to an old roller, repeating pattern in upholstery or drapery fabric.

Control light and privacy with upside-down shade

Floor-to-ceiling windows pose problems of privacy. Simple, effective solution is to install colorful shades upside down. Fasten the pulleys to the top of the window frame, grommets to top of shade, as shown below.

Two cords run through pulleys can be secured by a small peg at the side.

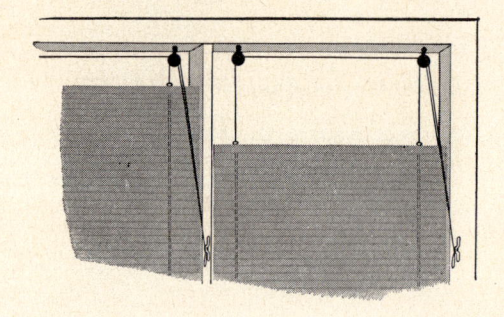

Felt shades and curtains add masculine air to boy's room or den

There's no need to sew hems here—just cut felt right size to fit your windows. Stitch on several rows of colorful braid to make the stripes. Staple shades to your old rollers. Cut matching scalloped curtains for the sides, trim them and make loops for hanging from the same braid you used on the shades.

Combine cafe curtains and pull-down shades for decorative effect

Sun- and spot-resistant fiberglass makes these brightly patterned shades practical. When soiled, just dip them in soapy water, rinse, hang.

Cafe curtains in a solid color are a soft background for the furniture arrangement. Colors pick up tones of the patterned floor covering.

Bright color, soft lines of Austrian shade are center of interest →

Like a stage curtain raised on a setting is an Austrian shade for a window that opens on a striking view.

Do-it-yourself kits are on the market, including cords and rings so you can make a shade like this from fabric that matches your decor. A lightweight material's best.

Woven wood blind sets a color scheme

There's new beauty in blinds. You can choose from wood slats with alternating plastic strips, or with a special bevel that cuts light, lets air circulate.

New matchstick bamboo comes in colors and patterns—or spray your own. Classic Venetians can be hung vertically, operate like draw draperies. Some have overlapping slats, really darken rooms.

Before you shop, measure windows accurately. For separate blinds on casement windows and French doors, measure glass, then add two inches to length, width. If blinds are to be set inside casing, measure the inside exactly, let the store tell you what size to buy. If blinds go outside woodwork, measure width between outside edges of frames. Measure length from top of frame to apron or floor. Measure wall space you want covered at sides and top of window.

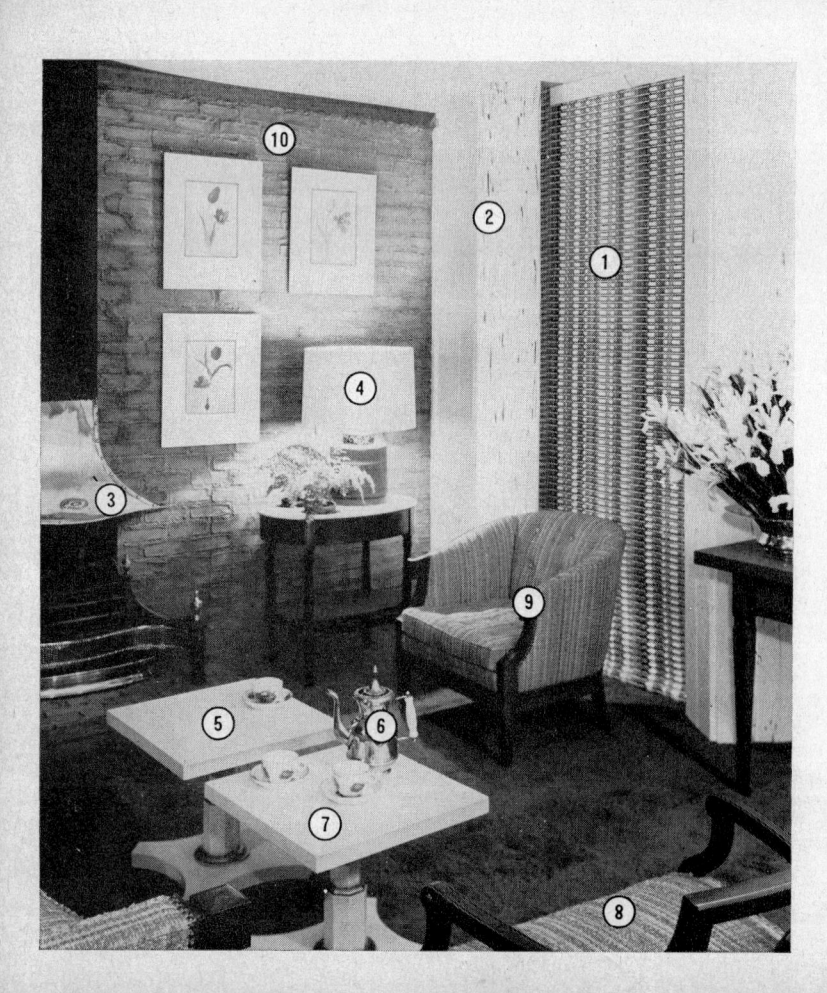

A wood-slat blind, woven with rough yarns and metal threads, sets the decorating theme here. Its colors and textures are picked up and blended with all the rest of the room's furnishings. Other ideas to adapt:

1. The blind gains importance, serves as a wall decoration too, hung from ceiling to floor. It hides a narrow, too-high window.

2. Ceiling-to-floor shutters are used instead of draperies to control privacy. These are of pecky cypress rubbed with white to blend with wall.
   Yours could be panels of plywood, put together with piano hinges, and painted to match the wall. If you use neither shutters nor draperies, you will probably need a room-darkening shade underneath the blind.

3. Fireplace hood is lower than usual. You gain a high-ceiling look in an average room when the furniture is kept low, close to floor.

4. Three big pictures and the lamp shade are arranged in a group.
   A small room looks less cluttered when furniture and wall decorations fit into a pattern. It's wise to sketch heights of furniture pieces on a floor-wall plan, take it with you when shopping so you can choose right sizes and shapes.

5. Twin tables fit together as one big table, or pull apart to serve chairs separately. You could make your own with pedestals from secondhand or lumber store, top them with plywood covered with plastic.

6. Blend metal tones for a unified look. Here, the bright brass coffeepot, the flower bowl, even the trim on the tables, reflect the gleam of the fireplace hood and fender.

7. White in mass—pull-up tables, wall, shutters, pictures and frames, marble-topped table—make warm tones look even warmer, friendlier.

8. One fabric on all the upholstered pieces pulls the room together without monotony, blends with the tones of brick, blind, wood, carpet.

9. Look for wood arms on upholstered pieces that get a lot of family use. Wood is at the spots where hands usually grip, keeps upholstery looking better, wearing longer.

10. Plan for texture interest. Here rough brick and blind are foils for smooth walls, gleaming brass.
    Instead of a brick wall you might like a simulated three-dimensional wall covering, burlap, or grass cloth.

45

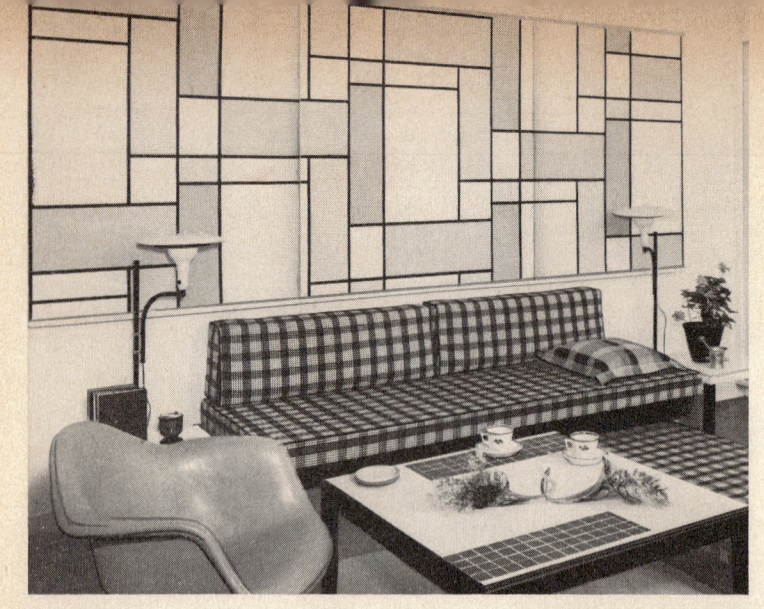

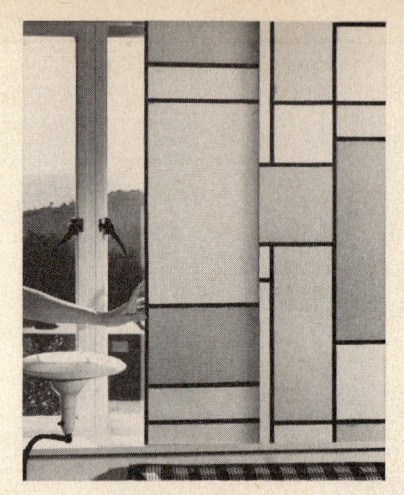

Sliding panels are both a window cover-up and a contemporary wall design

Badly placed windows are at either end of this wall. Clever treatment put them behind sliding panels that were covered with a geometrical abstraction, bringing striking color and design into an otherwise simply decorated room. Two side panels slide behind central one which is stationary when you want to admit light and air. Plywood—light in weight, easy to handle—is the material of which the sliding panels are constructed.

Cover up with sliding panels

Windows aren't always where we'd like them. They may be awkward in size or lack a view. One way to meet these challenges is to disguise them.

Since panels take little space, don't open in, they offer no furniture arrangement problems. You can play them down by painting in wall color, or feature them with bold color and pattern.

Hide a window, create a view

This window had no view and its characterless original treatment included a useless window seat.

This was ripped out, shoji panels installed, and "view" created with graceful foliage. Old jog in the wall was enclosed to produce handsome and useful built-in storage.

Tiers of shutters give importance to a window of only ordinary dimensions

On a long wall, this window looked too small. It gained size and beauty with three tiers of shutters.

Top bank is kept closed over a bare wall; bottom and center sections open or close, as desired.

Camouflage with shutters

Shutters deserve their long-time popularity because they require little upkeep, look well with almost any style of furnishings, add distinction.

Easily operated, they let you open up as many sections as you like, for a small amount or a maximum of sunlight. Paint or paper them so as to camouflage or dramatize window placement.

Shutters covered in the wallpaper pattern let window blend into the wall

Problem: How can we play down a window that would distract from effect of a boldly patterned wallpaper?

Solution: De-emphasize opening by installing shutter covered with the paper. Careful match disguises lines.

Unobtrusive china knobs protect paper from soil. As an alternative, you might choose a washable wallpaper, or use a special protective spray coat.

Try one of these ways with cafes

Whether your choice of furnishings is Traditional or Contemporary, elegant or simple, there's an adaptation of cafe curtains that is suitable.

Originally used at restaurant windows—hence their name—cafe curtains offer flexibility and privacy. They usually hang by tabs or rings from a fixed rod, are often installed in tiers.

If tiered, set upper rods to project a bit, so lower curtains will not have a bunched look.

Control fullness with drawstrings below peaks

Gather the drawstrings as tightly as you wish for hanging; for easy ironing, release them so curtains will lie flat. Metal clasps fasten cafes to pole, make it easy to open or close.

To control light at the top, roll blinds make suitable companions for tailored cafe curtains.

Cafe curtains with folding shutters look authentic in a provincial scheme

Another way to get extra fullness in cafes is demonstrated in these pumpkin color curtains that match bedspreads and canopies. Pinch pleats below each peak are handled in much the same manner as for conventional draperies, with a half-circle cut out between each group of pleats for the cafe effect.

← Fabric shade to match cafe curtains

News here is matched fabric in shades and cafes.

In a more informal room, accompanying draw draperies could be dispensed with.

Here, the three-way combination gives maximum flexibility of light control.

Border cafes with fabric to match paper

If your wallpaper has a matching fabric, use it to border curtains, give a custom air.

If the pattern is large, applique individual motifs on the panels. Combine longer cafes with a deep ruffle to shut out view, let in light.

Draperies advance color and style of room schemes

The view through a window wall is often the eye-catching, dramatic point around which your decorating revolves. But you need draperies, too, to control glare and supply nighttime privacy.

Take advantage of this wonderful expanse of fabric to make a wall that's as interesting with draperies closed as open.

If you have a series of small windows, you can get the effect by draping the entire wall. For corner windows, run draperies across one wall, around the corner.

Stripes give a high-ceilinged look

Mostly chalk white, these draperies sharpen the appeal of a subtle color scheme. They are given individuality through narrow vertical bands that repeat soft yellow of walls and room accents.

Delicate pastels set the decorating theme

Gauze panels in three blending colors are stitched together to emphasize the color scheme. You can have privacy and protection, too, with separate insulated lining that travels on its own rod. Metallic coating repels summer sun, retains winter heat.

Cover a corner, dramatize a wall

Floor-to-ceiling, wall-to-wall, a patterned fabric sets the accent colors here, pulls to the right to uncover a corner window. Matching material in plain white blends with the wall color, pulls to the left.

Tailored treatments help disguise radiators

A great many older homes have at least one window under which, or next to which rests a necessary but ugly radiator that presents problems of window treatment.

With a combination of a stylish radiator cover and draperies tailored to clear the top, you can effectively distract attention from the offending radiator—perhaps even make an asset of it, if you're clever.

If your radiator is centered under a window, include it in your window treatment. If it stands alone at one side of the room, extend the treatment to include it, as has been done in the room at left.

When boxing in a radiator, it's important to provide at least a three-inch space at the top, for circulation of heat and air.

Storage unit's an extension of cover

A tall radiator was placed at right of window. Shutter-pattern wallpaper suggested real shutters to cover it, extend to form a window seat and storage cabinet. The shutters could be custom-, ready-made, or used ones.

Turn radiators into simple window seats

Radiator covers are painted to match the walls, topped with seat cushions. Draw draperies meet the cushion. Separate panels of the same fabric extend to the floor at the sides, tie treatment together into a unit.

Chapter four

Decorating ideas for furniture arrangement

Move furniture on paper—it's easier than doing it physically. Start with a floor plan. It can serve as a shopping guide, show you just the colors and sizes you need.
1. Make a floor plan, indicating location of doors, windows, electrical outlets.
2. Establish your traffic patterns—the obvious paths people will take to get into, out of, and across a room.
3. Find your center of decorating interest —a fireplace, a long wall, a view.
4. Place your furniture on floor plan. Use a Better Homes & Gardens furniture arrangement kit, as illustrated, or draw your own to scale on ruled paper.
5. Plan location of color and pattern. Keep in mind over-all distribution of both.

Six tips for arranging furniture

1. It is perfectly correct to place furniture out in a room, away from walls. But if you do, install a floor outlet for lamps—don't leave dangerous cords to trip over which are plugged into a faraway wall.
2. Place furniture groupings so traffic goes around, not through them.
3. Keep chairs close enough together so people don't have to shout across a room. Maximum of eight feet between groupings is most pleasant and comfortable.
4. Leave at least a 30-inch traffic lane for passing between furniture groupings; more if you'll be carrying trays or any kind of game equipment through.
5. A table should be about the same height as the arm of its sofa or chair. It looks better, avoids spills and upset lamps.
6. Select table first; then accompanying lamp. Know table height when you shop and choose lamp height accordingly.

First, sketch your floor plan to scale

Use graph paper, letting one square equal a square foot. Draw room outline accurately. Show location and sizes of windows, doors, electrical outlets.

Plan placement and color distribution →

After you've established the traffic patterns, move paper furniture outlines around until you have a good placement. Then plan for your colors.

Plan comfortable seating space near the television

Even if you have a selector system, you'll probably want to adjust television tuning yourself from time to time. Place a chair near the set for comfort.

Make the set an integral, unobtrusive part of your decorating; incorporate it in a grouping. Here, chairs, mirror, and pictures keep it company.

Slim pieces perform well, take minimum wall space

A long, shallow desk has plenty of working space and drawer room, conserves floor space, too. Off-the-floor construction makes it easier to clean carpeting.

Shelves and hanging light provide library convenience. Colorful area rug sets the space apart. Always place furniture on or off a rug . . . never half on, half off.

Slim furniture

Bookcases and slim table make a useful reading-writing center

Built-in bookcases, a modern revival of the old library table, a pull-up chair convert this corner into usable space. The large lamp gives good reading light for the table; serves sofa, too.

Color, furniture scale and arrangement combine for maximum use of den-guest room

Shallower than conventional sofas, these convert to guest beds by removing cushions. The low chest for guest storage is also a convenient end table.

Using white both for background and furnishings increases a spacious look. The deep tone of coffee table and motifs in white rug provide necessary contrast.

conserves space

If you're looking for extra living space, take advantage of optical illusion. It's relatively simple to fool the eye on matters of size: light-scale furniture will make a room seem appreciably larger; so will pale, solid colors. And good lighting, too, helps increase space visually.

Designers of Contemporary furniture are your allies in a search for space. Slim legs, see-through qualities such as you find in the desk chairs pictured on these pages, and straight lines all contribute to a space-making appearance.

You needn't veto pattern entirely; just use it judiciously if space is limited, for nothing eats space faster than large, all-over patterns. Instead, rely on the widely-spaced pattern such as you see in the white rug below; or count on subdued plaids or narrow stripes for contrast.

Narrow desk helps define an entry and separates living area

A desk which takes little actual space seems even smaller because of its open design. It does double duty as a divider of space and a handy household office.

Inexpensive woven rugs sewed together in a runner increase separation of areas.

Desk-table gives free passage through traffic end of room

Well-chosen furniture makes this end of a living room useful without obstructing a necessary traffic lane.

The narrow table is both a desk and a buffet server when needed. Two low chairs will push under the table and out of the way when not in use. Or, they can easily be pulled into the room for extra guest seating.

Solid colors throughout increase the big-room look.

Two kinds of light plus panels divide large room

The sofa arrangement separates the two areas in this room, furthered by the series of see-through panels that stop the eye, yet let light pass from one section of the room to the other.

A clever use of lighting creates a divider effect, too. In the living area, suspended lanterns give diffused general lighting. In the dining area a recessed ceiling fixture sends light straight down.

Furniture designed to separate space, and an area rug function well as dividers

A feeling of openness is retained by means of the see-through dividers. Their design is echoed in that of chairs in both parts of the room.

Ceiling fixture spotlights the dining table, with lamps used for reading light in living area.

Feature the color scheme in a room divider

Create a hallway and announce your color theme, too, with a handsome homemade divider. This one is made of pre-coated Venetian blind slats interwoven between plastic clothesline, anchored top and bottom. Choose your own materials, include all the colors in your scheme.

Sofa, tall foliage plant divide areas

A curving sectional sofa is placed next to a slight wall jog so that its longest portion projects into the room and serves to separate the living and dining areas.

The division is further emphasized by placing a foliage plant to screen the dining area.

Decorate and separate with room dividers

There is a trend in architecture today to leave out walls, throw open large areas, give an impression of bigness, and devise rooms that are to be used for more than one purpose.

In such rooms, it's often desirable to use a divider of some sort to separate one activity from another. It may take the form of a piece of furniture, freestanding panels, area rugs, or it may amount merely to a change of color from one section of the room to another. As a subtle but effective reinforcement of any divider, vary the lighting that's used in the two room areas.

Space-making

It is true that pale colors make a room seem larger. But brilliant, thrusting tones can be used against light backgrounds in a tiny space if you hold to straight lines, keep to pieces that are small in scale, not flouncy in their outlines.

If you prefer medium tones, use blending colors, play texture against texture for greater interest.

← Blending wood tones camouflage size

The handsome storage piece and sectioned screen in this dining room have large scale, but their bulk is disguised since the dark finish and fabric colors blend into color and finish of paneling.

Because they are camouflaged, they seem in keeping with the lightly scaled dining table and chairs.

Slim lines counteract use of vivid hues

Straight, slender lines of furnishings used in a small space permit the use of brilliant red and blue without an overcrowded look resulting.

Pure white walls help to expand space visually. And so does the use of cushioned pads on a bench, in place of a bulky overstuffed armchair.

You could make an impressive screen like the one above from discarded door panels, or by building a frame, finishing to harmonize with furniture tones.

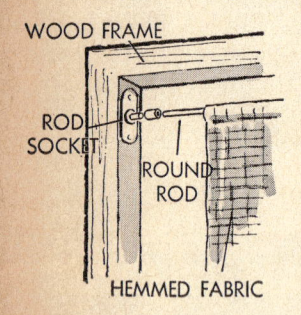

Fit the curtain rods into sockets, top and bottom of the open part of the panels.

Choose fabric to suit the decorating scheme. Hem at sides if necessary, then at top and bottom, with slot wide enough to take rods.

WOOD FRAME
ROD SOCKET
ROUND ROD
HEMMED FABRIC

Inject dramatic and enlivening color in a → room scheme with a floor-to-ceiling screen. This one is made of plywood panels, painted white, and then covered with strips of leather. Brass-headed upholstery tacks, closely spaced give a professional finish. Cover might be of felt, grass cloth, some leather-like plastic, or strips of fabric used on chairs or for draperies.

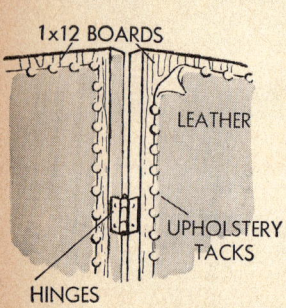

1x12 BOARDS
LEATHER
UPHOLSTERY TACKS
HINGES

depends upon color, line and scale

Small pattern, pale colors, light scale furniture give sense of space

A small sitting room seems bigger than it is because of the way it's decorated. Light colors account for much of the spacious effect; contributing, too, is dainty, all-over print that bulks smaller visually than a large print. Furniture of slender scale leaves space for movement about the room.

An informal balance creates a casual air

This informal room with its Traditional furnishings has a friendly look that's partly due to furniture arrangement. A lightly scaled wing chair and cane-backed rocker make a congenial pair.

Informal balance is used again for the grouping of mantel decorations.

Built-in shelves beside the window form a unit in visual balance with chair and tray at the left of the fireplace opening.

Arrangement gives a unified appearance

The bulk of the wing chair, table and lamp group at the right is balanced by another chair and table grouping at the left. Centered and framed by the windows and chairs is the handsome secretary desk.

This placement is a space-saving idea

If you have a sectional sofa or love seat, but not enough room for tables at each end, separate halves and put a single table and tall lamp between them. Unite grouping with a decorative wall treatment.

Hanging table between two chairs releases floor space for extra stools

In this narrow room, the problem was to find a comfortable arrangement that would still permit traffic to pass, give extra seating in minimum space.

The covers of the two lounge chairs were blended to the wall color to minimize their size. A hanging shelf, its sturdy chains framing the tall lamp, leaves floor space free.

Two square stools are stored here, their covers picking up the accent colors of the room. They are easy to pull out and use when extra seating is needed.

Find the right chair arrangement for your room

There's nothing more inviting than two or three chairs drawn up together in a friendly conversation group. A table within easy reach, and a good light for reading add comfort and appeal.

The "extra" chairs—the ones you need for company, but not for everyday living—should be part of your furnishings plan.

Choose dining room chairs that can serve as occasional seating, too, blending in color and style with the rest of your furniture. Buy one or two more than you need for dining purposes and use them at desk or telephone stand. Pull them into conversation group when company comes.

Team chairs with chest for decorative unit

Occasional chairs are just that—for occasions when you need them, but not for everyday. Combine them with other pieces of furniture to make an interesting arrangement. Bring them out into conversation grouping when needed.

Two chairs and a table form a room divider

Not needed for everyday family use, but ready for guests, this table-chair grouping separates through traffic lane from the living room proper. Other matching chairs, at desk and against wall, can also be brought into the circle.

Chapter five

Decorating ideas for living rooms

Your living room is frequently a keystone to your decorating plan . . . the room from which colors are taken for other rooms.

It's traditionally the room that first welcomes guests . . . the spot where a family lives together. Decorate it to suit your own tastes, to include colors and kinds of furnishings you like best. Here are points to keep in mind as you plan:
1. Make a floor and color plan first.
2. Take the plan with you when you shop.
3. Blend colors; don't try to match them exactly. Differing textures will vary the appearance of colors considerably.
4. Look at color samples under the same light as in the room where they'll be used. Check them both by day and by lamp light.
5. Plan lighting so that at least some of it comes from the same direction as does natural light from your windows.
6. Check information tags on upholstered furniture to learn the fiber content, how best to care for the particular fabric.
7. Choose your carpet according to kind of wear it will get. Heavy traffic requires better quality, footprint-hiding texture, color that doesn't easily show soil.

If Contemporary is your choice, look for basic shapes that enrich smaller homes

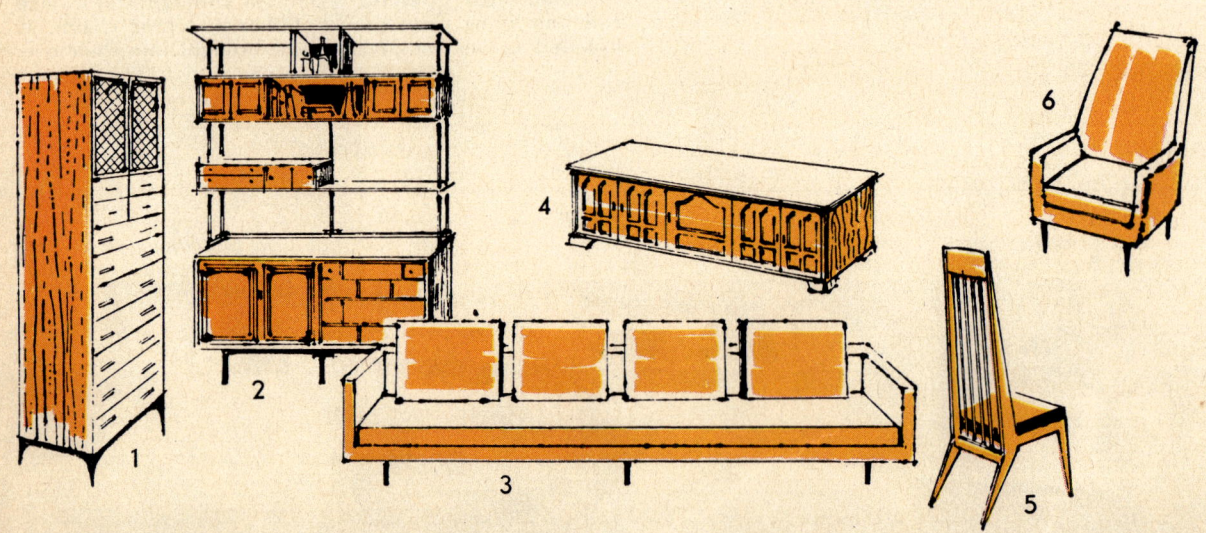

1 and 2. Storage pieces climb the wall, measure as much as seven feet tall. Less open shelving, more hideaway space, give uncluttered look. 3 and 4. Low ceilings, window walls, ask for a long, low look. Sofas stretch out to fill a wall; bench tables, low chests, are often six feet long. 5 and 6. Choose some tall pieces to balance the low look. Slim headrest and pull-up chairs can look considerably taller than their actual height.

Thoughtful planning can bring a new look with every change of season

In warmer weather, push the chairs and bench back to the fireplace wall, fill the opening with greens. Change slip covers and candles to a cool green, reflecting a tone in picture.

Decorative room accents can lend an air of individuality

Paste-on borders are easy way to inexpensive luxury

To give a room a whole new face at budget prices, few decorating devices offer greater possibilities than scenic and mural wall coverings or paste-on borders like these.

Sophisticated choice is black lamp shades to underscore the use of black elsewhere in this room.

Paint a chair for color accent and repeat the color elsewhere

It's Contemporary fashion and historical accuracy to paint chairs. Colonial favorites were brick red, black, or dark green. The mantel arrangement breaks the vertical lines of the wall; attention focuses on the fireplace. Rug touches the hearth, but leaves exposed floor border around the room.

Knotty pine, stained with color, makes an imaginative wall treatment

To imitate a decorating scheme like this one, stain the wood paneled walls first, then choose blending color for painted areas. Woods vary; stain color may not be completely predictable. Red fabric of upholstery and accent pillows heightens color of terra cotta brick, adds life, and warmth.

Color and texture combine to give a room its personality

Floors here were in bad repair; plaster walls were cracked. Owner chose to put his money in wall-to-wall carpeting, covered hall in dark grass cloth, complementing color, texture of brick wall.

Brass curtain rod runs from the fireplace to end wall, supplies privacy and background for chair.

Lamp on television set serves chair and reduces glare, eyestrain when the set is in use.

Five decorating ideas you can copy for a room with a view

1. Drapery covering door is welcoming note, repeats color of the chair and cushions in living area to relate these sections.
2. Beams are stained the same color indoors and out to strengthen a sense of indoor-outdoor living.
3. Divider between areas is high enough to serve as a sofa wall, low enough to preserve a desirable openness of feeling.
4. Pictures at far end of room are hung high enough to be seen through the room divider when seated in the living area.
5. Furniture is arranged to capitalize on the garden scene; sofa and white chair face the window; chair and table group are low and placed to one side so as not to obstruct the outdoor view.

Renting—or building a new home? Buy furnishings that will move with you

Sectional furniture of the type used here is a wise purchase if you contemplate a move. Sectional sofa at far end of room could go around a corner; cabinets and shelves might be rearranged to include a desk; sofa and table combination might be placed in several other ways in different settings.

Pre-finished panels, unfinished cabinets create an orderly, useful wall arrangement

Before: Dull and undistinguished, room needed order and interest. *After* (right): carefully selected to size, unfinished cabinets were stained to blend with paneling. Valance lighting spots treasures.

1. Living and dining areas are separated only by the exposed ceiling beams and pull-up chairs used as a divider. They are closely united through the style and finish of furniture, as well as by the identical floor covering in both rooms.

2. Good color distribution is achieved by echoing the red of the lounge chair in toss pillows across the room.

3. Use of one color on ceiling and walls helps to unify the room. If ceilings are low, use a light tint or white.

4. Unmatched woods, including pine, fruitwood, maple and cherry, blend together happily since styles are compatible.

5. Furniture that moves easily is ideal for a combination living-dining room. The low coffee table in the foreground was made by shortening legs of a sofa table, adding casters so it can be rolled between the living and dining areas, serve both rooms. The captain's chairs are light enough to be moved about easily for dinner or for an evening of conversation.

6. Interchangeable rugs mean longer wear. Although the living section is somewhat larger than the dining area, the two rugs are cut exactly the same size. They can be alternated to equalize wear near the doorways and the sofa.

7. Mobile lighting fixtures allow greater flexibility in lighting. Some move up and down like the drop light in foreground. Some change direction, like the spotlights on the pole.

8. Inside of china cabinet is painted a delicate tint of the blue-green which covers sofa. "Showcase" lights intensify color.

9. Pictures are hung in a carefully organized fashion, with the greens at left and the pewter on the mantel forming part of the composition. But the grouping has interesting variety—portraits in oil, Audubon prints, tinsel under glass, and even a street scene rendered in embroidery. Spotlight from pole lamp is directed so it illuminates the display.

10. Seat cushions add comfort to a wooden chair, but should be thin so chair doesn't become too high for dining. Cushions are upholstered in fabric which doesn't wrinkle or stretch.

11. Wooden benches play dual role, serve as tables or seats.

12. Rectangular basket holds magazines on bench in front of sofa. Move the whole stack at once when extra seating's needed.

This room has a

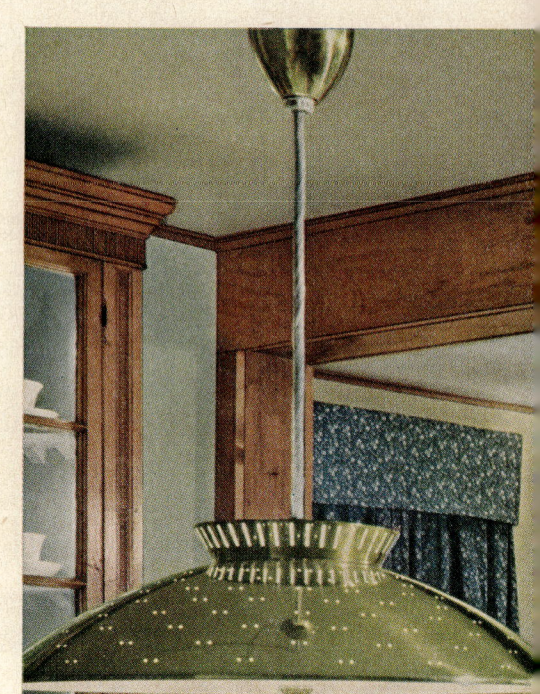

Ideas translate to any kind of room—for results you'll like, copy an idea, not the entire room

dozen decorating ideas you could adapt to your home

Color plan here is a box of white—ceiling, walls and rug; upholstery and drapery areas of a deep rich tone; balanced accents of bright red. Wood tones of furniture blend with paneled wall and beams.

When you group pictures in a unit, try to include some different shapes, such as the candlesticks and plate on the mantel. Easiest way to plan such a group is to cut paper shapes to same size as pictures and objects to be included. Fasten them to a painted or wood wall with masking tape, to a papered wall with pins. Move them about until you have the design you want.

Mark corners lightly with a pencil for easy hanging. Individual pieces can be in many media—prints, paintings, etc.,—but should be related in subject or style.

Carry accent color from room to room to attain co-ordination

Pinky-red upholstery on the living room sofa is especially pleasing against a neutral background. Using color again for valance and bench in hall beyond unites the areas.

Hall flooring is hard-surface and easy to keep clean. It's a clever idea to choose vinyl for traffic spots to match or contrast with the carpeting of adjacent areas.

Reverse a color scheme and co-ordinate two adjoining areas

Separate areas are related by floor treatment; wood finish blends with red tones. Bookcase and shutters furnish the window wall—could be the spot to hide air conditioner. Brick wall might be new heavy-duty wall covering that feels like brick, or less costly, gaily sham paper.

Tall sectional furniture gives the appearance of architectural built-in

Wood finish blends with floor and chair fabric. Corner desk has space below to hide a wastebasket or a portable typewriter case. Effect of brick floor could be gained with a brick-patterned linoleum. Curtain rod lines up with window crossbar. Opaque lamp shade is right height to shield eyes.

Complement contemporary furnishings with color

This homeowner is a designer of modern furniture who likes to couple its brilliant colors, sleek lines with the subdued intricacy of old pieces.

Under-the-window cabinet has marble inserts, is set out from windows to leave room for draperies to open without bunching up. Glass top makes it safe for a display of foliage plants, without fear of watermarks.

Hanging lights spotlight the richness of wood, call attention to carved wall plaque. Area rug defines the sofa-chair-coffee table grouping, and is related to off-whites and neturals of walls and draperies.

Lighting emphasizes dramatic architecture

Ceiling-installed spotlights focus on the shimmering length of a copper fireplace hood. Hanging fixtures and the skylight point up this room's unique appeal both in daytime and after dark.

Blue crossbeams accentuate the appeal of a high ceiling, reflect wall color of an adjoining room, and advance the color scheme initiated by upholstered furniture in Contemporary style which furnishes the room. Accents introduce a harmonious Oriental note.

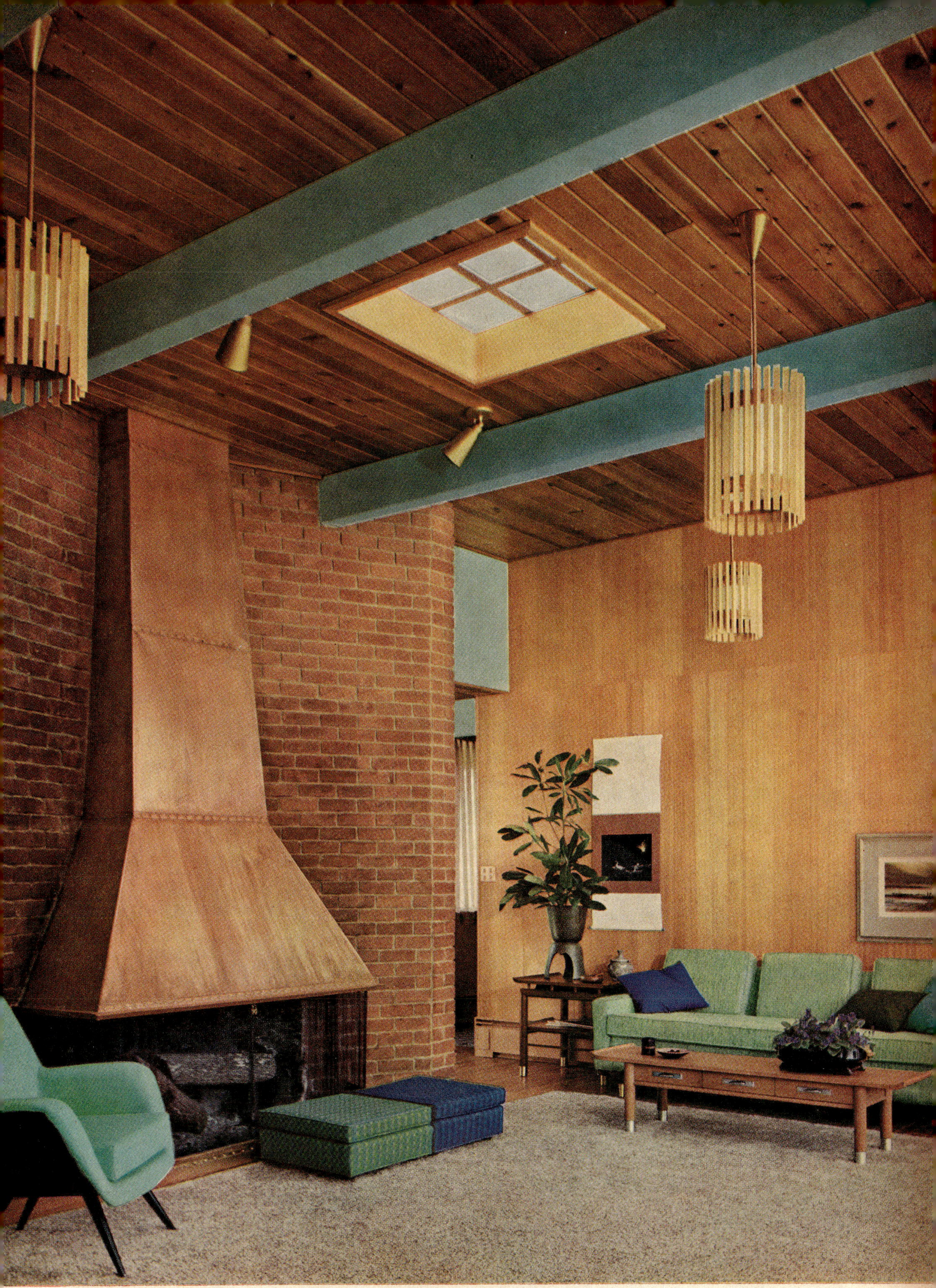

Area rugs solve room arrangement problems

Area rugs are especially useful in the new open plan houses, or in older homes with big rooms devoted to more than one use. They act as room dividers, separating two or more living areas.

In the room pictured at right, a sculptured oval rug takes the shape of the dining table. A rectangular rug defines the living area, helps unite a conversation grouping of furniture.

If you plan such a room, diagram your furniture plan first. You will see at once the size of rug to buy, the shape that will be most in harmony with the room's dimensions as well as its furnishings.

In either natural or synthetic fibers, small rugs permit economizing on size rather than quality. Easily moved, they're especially practical for the family contemplating relocation. New spot resistant fibers make light colors practical.

Besides the effective use of area rugs, this room includes other good decorating ideas:

1. Color balance is excellent. Chair seats in the dining room blend with sofa upholstery, can move into living room for extra party seating. Almost black upholstery of living room chairs repeats dark tone of stain on the desk chair. Blue which predominates in the dining room is brought into living area in form of accents.

2. Chandelier over the dining table includes a downward spot to focus on table decorations.

3. Closed china cabinet in dining room provides needed height, lots of hideaway storage.

4. Desk lamp is tall enough for good work light, also supplies over-all lighting for this end of the living room sofa and chair grouping.

5. Wall masks are hung so as to form a decorative unit that includes the lamp shade.

6. Living area furniture is placed so that traffic passes by, not through it. The dark chairs define a hall area out of view in picture.

Lighten masses of deep wood tones with large amounts of pale neutrals and accent with smaller but still important areas of bold color

The color plan began with a strong plaid whose tones blend with paneled wall of teak. Plaid colors were picked up for sofa, chair, and bench upholstery.

White with a fleck of green serves as hard-surface floor covering. Pure white appears in draperies and in picture frame and pole-lamp shade.

Although it looks costly, paneled wall comes in prefinished panels, four by eight feet, making it easy to install your own. The area rug was cut to follow shape of coffee table, with fringe dyed to match.

Pole lamp spots picture, helps general lighting. It is available in a variety of styles and finishes.

Good decorating capitalizes on architecture

Taking advantage of a seemingly pointless jog in the wall, these homeowners converted what might have been regarded as a handicap into an asset by building in floor-to-ceiling bookshelves that add convenience and interest to the room.

Other transforming changes that were inexpensive and simple include basic blue denim covers for the sofa and armchair; a bright felt cover glued to a plywood chair to make it an eye-catcher; antique bench, dressed up with blue cushion and teamed with a former dining table to produce an unusual desk and chair combination.

Call attention to a vaulted ceiling

Unique fixtures were improvised from the glass reflectors used in floor lamps, clustered to emphasize the sweep of the vaulted ceiling.

Beams are stained to blend with copper disks and still harmonize with greenish stain of walls and ceiling that lets brown tones shine through.

White lacquered cylinder under converted antique lamp base raises it to proper reading height, is related to the shade in its repetition of white . . . good idea to make old lamps taller.

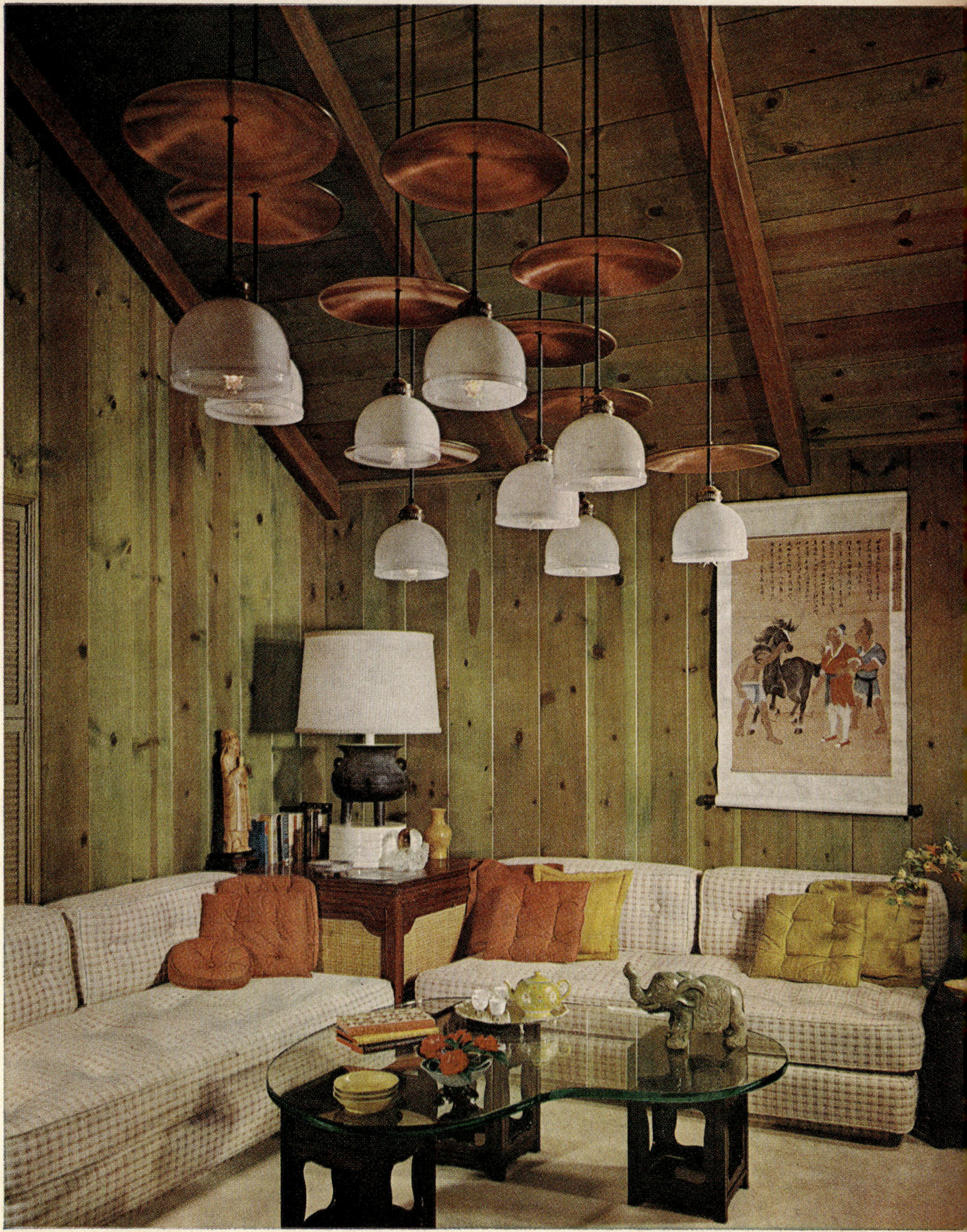

Consider color and scale in wall decor

In a low-ceilinged room, this picture grouping was designed to increase apparent wall height. Top row is hung only inches below the ceiling.

Black, gray and off-white tones of the prints preserve a basically neutral color scheme which uses vivid color only in limited amounts, as an accent, and employs a minimum of pattern.

If you have favorite black and white pictures you would like to hang in this manner, it's possible to have them photostatically reproduced in size you wish, mounted on hardboard, framed with or without glass. Keep frames thin for the best effect in a sizable grouping such as this.

Horizontal lines have a restful quality

Low lines of a Contemporary sofa and tables are exploited and emphasized by a narrow wall hanging running the full length of sofa.

You could copy this design or devise your own, executing it as a hooked pattern, applique, or with paints to suit the scale of your room.

Vertical strips of wood paneling on the end wall give welcome contrast, as does the extra tall lamp on the corner table.

Budget idea: make pillow pads like those in foreground to fit a simple, inexpensive bench.

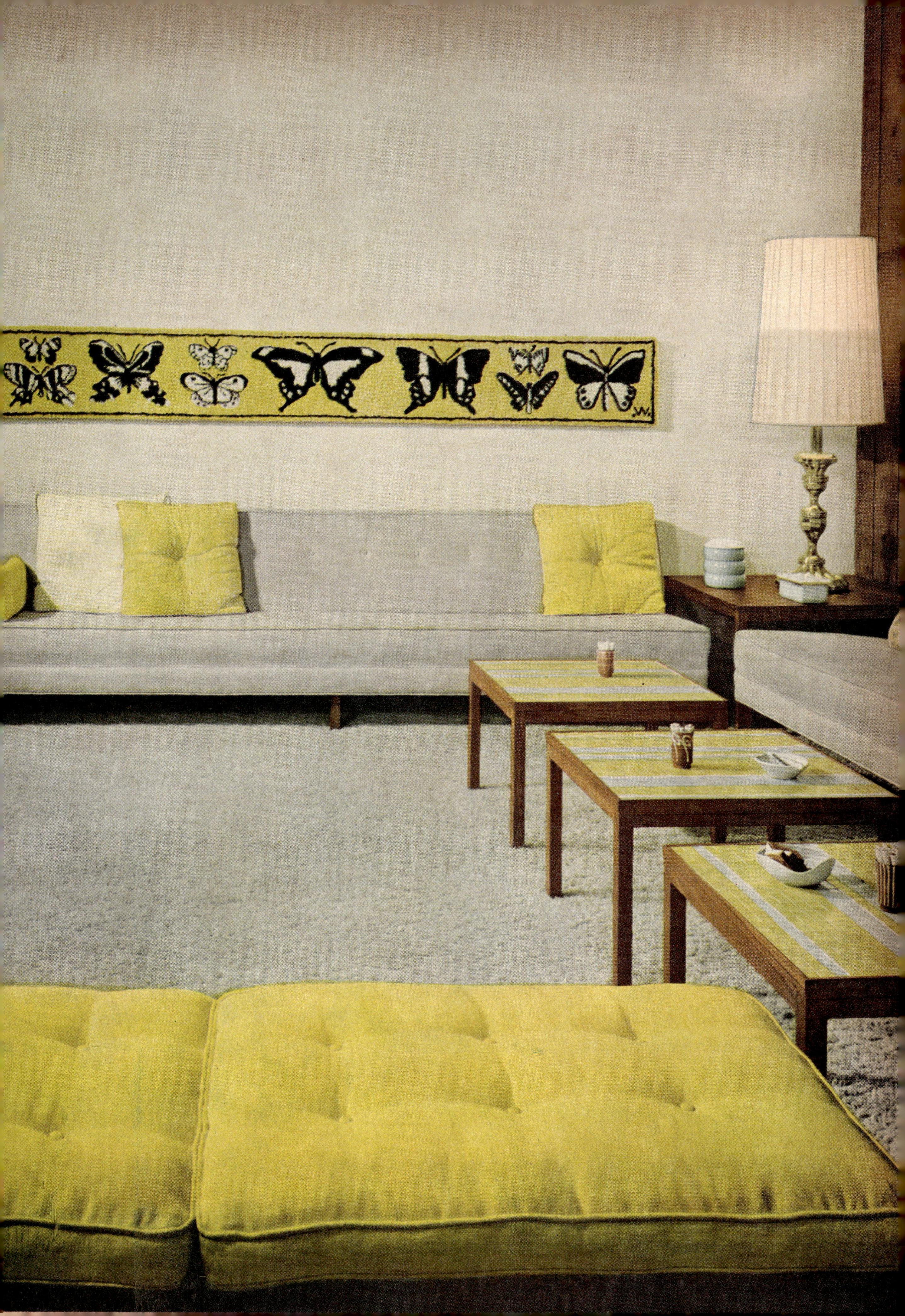

Chapter six

Decorating ideas for dining rooms

Dining rooms are often used just once a day . . . when the family gathers at dinnertime, or when you have guests. Plan its color scheme under lights like those you'll use, choose colors and textures for after-dark drama. Here are some points to consider:
1. If you display silver, set it against a cool color background. Warm tones like yellow will make it look tarnished, even when it has been freshly polished.
2. Look for floor covering that's easy to clean—you won't be able to avoid spills or spots.
3. Consider the new colored light bulbs for your fixtures—the rose ones particularly flatter both people and food.
4. Plan "good" and "everyday" dishes to blend with color scheme. You'll be able to mix them for parties without a thrown-together look.
5. If your table takes hard wear, look for woods with heat, stain- and water-resistant finishes, or for plastic tops that look like wood.

Create inviting backgrounds that reinforce the daily pleasures of dining

Create a combination dining-game room by screening off a big bay or the end of a long living room.
Consider resilient flooring —vinyl or linoleum—that blends in color with carpeting in the rest of the house. Pattern or mottled motifs will reduce upkeep time.
Folding screens or doors will let you shut off the space after a meal, tidy it up when guests have left.

There's no law that makes you place the dining table in the center of the room. To avoid an awkward traffic pattern, put it against a long wall; to take advantage of a view, set your dining table in front of a window.
Color scheme your linens to the general color plan of the room—or, match napkins to flower centerpiece, have contrasting cloths or mats for interest.

Plan for gentle, soft, over-all light—you do want your guests to be able to see their food. Plan, too, for direct light to spot the center of your table, or treasures displayed on the buffet.
A pull-down light makes the table convenient for study, homework, or games.
Choose colors and textures under the light where you will be using them.

Fragile-looking yet sturdy fabrics lend this area a garden air

So feminine and fresh, yet practical—curtains and tablecloth are wash-and-dry material that keeps its crispness; rug goes into the washer, tumbles dry; seats are plastic that wipes off.

Settings can turn a meal into a special occasion

Make room for activities other than dining by placing your table against a wall. Instead of legs, this table has an intriguing pedestal of angled walnut strips. It's attached to the wall for further security against tipping forward.

A handy man could duplicate the table top with a sheet of plywood covered with laminated plastic.

Wall hanging is a towel, framed by three lengths of bamboo.

Disguise architectural jogs with matching wallpaper and fabric

A small dining room gains traffic path by placing the table slightly off center. Other decorating ideas in the room worth copying:

1. Drop light that lets table be used for games or homework.
2. Chair seats that are copied after rug design. To make yourself, trace section of rug pattern on heavy paper, scale to size of the chair, transfer with carbon paper.
3. Storage cabinet has enclosed shelves, gives good hideaway space. Tall, shallow storage pieces are now available in sizes and shapes to fit most spaces.
4. Papered ceiling in bay area makes decorative unit of window.

*Add a family room
by rearranging your
big dining room*

An off-center arrangement gives plenty of space for all the family activities, leaves room for television, record player, and teen-age dancing. Other ideas:

1. Light comes from two sources: pull-down fixture that serves for study or cards; valance fixture for reading light at bench.

2. Built-in bench has storage drawers, could hide a difficult radiator, or an air conditioner.

3. Tier curtains adjust for privacy. Draw draperies at large window open to show view, give light for daytime reading or sewing.

*Wall decoration
sets a color theme
for the dining room*

Colors in the wall hanging reflect the warm wood tones of paneling and furniture, adding blue shades for contrast. Tones of the blue were picked up for the chair upholstery, the mats and china service.

If you'd like to make a wall hanging on this order, trace a design you like, transfer it to backing material for a rug. Hook and hang on your wall.

If you aren't adept at rug hooking, similar effects can be gained with cutouts of construction paper, or with paints.

The table is placed near enough to buffet for easy service, but far enough into room so that there is adequate passage.

Imaginative details stamp the seal of your taste on dining space

Document wallpaper print and paper dado give a boxy little room an authentic period feeling.

You could design a dado with picture molding fastened to wall, painted. Dado and draperies pick up blue and green notes in carpet. Painted chairs with rush seats add to "circa 1800" look.

Use sham brick to accent one or two walls, never on all four. It's available in three-dimensional plastic, or printed on paper. Remember—it's not fireproof, so don't use it near a flame.

Country-house air is emphasized by spattered floor covering, shutters. The brilliant color of table and chairs can be easily changed with a new paint job when you switch schemes.

Even a small pull-up server helps keep the dining table uncrowded

The charcoal stove-server here is an antique—you might use any small stand, add a warming unit. Idea to copy: Re-cover chair seats in a gay color drawn from your china, get napkins to harmonize. Try interesting shapes such as these knotted napkins.

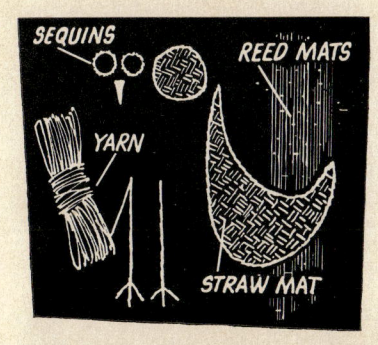

An inexpensive reed mat of the type sold for beach use makes a good background, or substitute burlap or monk's cloth.

First, cut out bird shapes on paper, arrange the pattern you want on the background. Trace the positions with a pencil, so you'll know where the finished pieces are to go.

Next, cut birds out of inexpensive straw table mats, varying color and texture. Paint neutral mats if you can't find colors you want. Glue to background.

Use yarn or pipe cleaners for legs and feet; sequins for eyes; felt for beaks; bits of glitter for crests and topknots.

Pose a flock of straw birds against a reed mat background

Fun to make ... fun to look at ... design your own "primitive" art to go into a Contemporary dining room. Secret of success is to make it big enough to be impressive. Don't worry about art technique. It should look hand-crafted.

Brighten a small room with sharp color against a neutral background

Secondhand furniture, a few yards of inexpensive fabric, a bucket of paint, elbow grease ... this was the formula for this sparkling room.

Tiny space dictated light walls. Furniture was cleaned thoroughly, painted to match. Chair seats echo a color in the picture, can be changed if color scheme changes.

The shelf below the window serves as a buffet. Serving cart rolls to kitchen, then under shelf for storage.

Use colors that contrast to give a room style

Brilliant jewel-toned floor-to-ceiling draperies hide little, uninteresting windows. Deep walls require a lot of light to show off the colors of the room.

Best solution would be ceiling spots, or series of recessed ceiling fixtures, spaced so tables can be shifted, still have beams of light directed downward on them.

Old restaurant tables with marble tops acquire elegance because of their setting. They can be grouped as one big table, used independently, or placed in a row for an intimate buffet. Rainbow hues of chair seat pads reflect colors of spatter linoleum used as floor covering. Hard-surface floors add to convenience if dining arrangements involve moving furniture.

Rejuvenate a room with a mural

A tiny dining room gets color from a floral mural reflecting graceful lines of metal furniture.

It's all so practical, too: papered wall is washable; filmy curtains require no ironing; even the chair covers are made of plastic fabric that wipes clean with a damp cloth.

Enlarge a small room, gain a gay background for informal dining

A refectory table goes across a long wall, is a perfect spot for family meals, or a fine buffet for guests. Table-setting colors come from view-stretching wallpaper mural.

Vinyl covering of chair seats harmonizes with bright tone of the floor covering. Cafe curtains in tiers temper the light, are quickly adjusted for greater privacy at mealtime.

Emphasize the elegant lines of old furniture with bright color . . . continue the mood of fantasy with a mural paper

Several different styles, periods blend into a happy unit when color is used with a lavish hand. Old chairs were refurbished with a coat of bright paint, covered in a softly golden fabric. The impressive round table was contrived from an old base, a new and elegant marble top.

Round rug repeats colors from the wallpaper mural, underscores the lines of the table. You could design your own to go with your color scheme, have it cut and sewed by your carpet retailer.

Color and pattern create illusions of space and depth in a small room

Gain a "dining *alfresco*" illusion in the tiniest of rooms with a wallpaper of balcony, balustrade and landscape motif. Pale blue and white help to create a feeling of spaciousness.

For a closet or storage cabinet, careful matching of the mural pattern will let you cover the doors so that the breaks scarcely show.

Metal chairs harmonize in color and motif with the wallpaper.

Four floor tiles of same color are used together for each square of checkerboard floor pattern that simulates marble.

Wire sculpture casts interesting shadows

Handyman art takes the form of metal sculpture that casts subtle shadows. First, draw a pattern; cut large pieces from copper sheet; use wire and BB's for small details; solder pieces together. Screw sculpture to wall through washer attached to back.

Floor tile pattern separates dining area

Staggered tiles form a transition, shading from off-white in dining area to solid brown in living end of room. You could copy idea for divider between hall and living room, using footprint-hiding shades in traffic areas, delicate hues in others.

Custom wall planned of bright color strips

Stripes are grass cloth cut in random widths, with plain gold on other walls. Flooring pattern is made from vinyl tiles laid on double-faced tape. They're firm and tight, but can be moved to another home, won't mar a wood floor. Slim legs give the storage cabinets a light look.

Furniture decoration is keyed to period

Painted-on decorative motifs in gold are suited to the classical design of this furniture.

A buffet table like this could be built to fit a salvaged slate or marble top, or top could be of plywood covered with a thermoset plastic.

Draperies turn a corner to cover a window or a storage cabinet

Floor-to-ceiling draperies turn a corner to define a dining area. Short side could cover open storage shelves, should pull from the left with separate cords.

Woods of wall paneling, furniture and floor blend in tone. The flooring is of pre-finished parquet blocks you could install.

Cantilevered storage cabinet leaves plenty of space for pull-up stools to be stored beneath.

Chapter seven

Decorating ideas for kitchens

Comfort and convenience are the two most important ingredients of your kitchen decorating . . . comfort in good lighting, in pleasing colors, in well-routed work . . . convenience in storage, in appliances. Here are some points to consider:
1. Install direct light sources over each working area—range, sink, et cetera.
2. Use flattering light over eating areas, make food more attractive.
3. Mottled or patterned floor covering requires less upkeep than solid colors.
4. Consider a soft underlayment for resilient floorings—give your feet a rest.
5. There's always steam in a kitchen—choose fabrics that won't shrink, stretch.
6. Plan a color scheme with some vibrant tones—this is one room where you want to be stimulated, keep awake.
7. Provide a comfortable stool, so you can sit at food preparation.
8. In a large kitchen, use a rolling cart as island server and work counter. Push it around with you from one work area to another, save steps and time.

Plan height and placement of appliances to fit your individual working pattern

← If your remodeling will include a built-in oven, do have it installed at the most comfortable height.
 A good rule-of-thumb is that the top of the opened oven door should be about three inches below the bend of your elbow.
 Provide for counter space near by so there's a landing spot for hot dishes.

Handy storage for every-day → appliances could be built by a handy man, or organized from a series of ready-made, unfinished cabinets.
 Counter height should be based on *your* height, whether you stand or sit to work. Add a chair for comfort.
 Add wheels to unit and use it as a roving island counter. Plug cord and electrical outlet would make it even more convenient.

↑ An indoor barbecue grill gets year-round use in family kitchens. When weather's nice, a portable cart wheels barbecued foods outdoors to terrace. Or, "picnics" can be served indoors any time.
 Built-in grills must be ventilated with exhaust fan and hood. Installation of ventilation system is easier when grill is set close to other cooking helpers. Or, place it in fireplace wall.

Combine old things with new to give a kitchen flair, personality

Problem: How to get a period look into a shiny modern kitchen. Solution: Use antiques. Fixture over marble island was a skylight, now turned upside down, fitted with lights above, Victorian hanging baskets below. Discarded hot-air registers make unusual doors at sink cabinet, also hide ugly radiator.

Kitchen windows can set decorating theme

← Checked denim cafe curtains topped with an awning-like cornice in matching material afford privacy while eating, yet let the light in. Cafes may be pulled aside if desired.

Support is made from two long brass curtain rods each bent into U shape. Rods are threaded through casings which are sewed onto the top and bottom of the fabric.

Favorite family vacation spot inspires a window treatment

Plastic grillwork combined with cotton lace cafes bring a touch of New Orleans to add charm to your kitchen eating area. →

Spring curtain rod for cafes is set at lower tip of grillwork. For easy installation attach the corner filigree to the steel casement frames with a plastic adhesive.

Sliding screens form a wall, point up the color scheme

A wall made of sliding screens forms a colorful background for this kitchen eating area. The screens are made of fir plywood painted red and faced with translucent plastic.

Every inch of precious space has been put to good use. The panels not only define the eating area but also conceal from view a washer, dryer, and extra clothes closet.

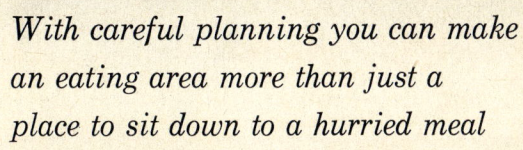

With careful planning you can make an eating area more than just a place to sit down to a hurried meal

If yours is a more formal home, carry the same theme into the kitchen with a Regency inspired window treatment and decorative accessories.

Greek-key braid is stitched to the sheer ready-made curtains covering window. A swag of another longer-length panel is draped through a pair of brass towel rings. Wrought iron furniture and brick-textured wall covering add to elegant feeling. Bench is covered with easy-to-keep-clean vinyl.

Matchstick bamboo in bright colors works wonders in kitchen decor, doesn't strain a decorating budget

← Pink, orange and purple matchstick panels add a spicy Oriental flavor to white-walled kitchen. Cut panels, then fit them to frames. Hinge frames together at top and bottom.

The matchstick bamboo panels filter light at the window; used on the cupboard doors they conceal china and tableware storage.

Pattern and color aid in revamping your kitchen scheme

A coat of paint, new porcelain knobs and a little yellow trim give this cabinet a new lease on life. Four casters were added so it could be moved about the kitchen easily, serve many purposes.

A side-attached knife rack, towel ring and electric outlet add usefulness. Old top is covered with vinyl.

Kitchen stool's an old highchair that has had its arms and tray removed, then painted. Foam cushion was slip-covered in washable print. Fringe was added to the pad and wastebasket.

Multi-colored paper in harlequin design defines eating area

Patterned wallpaper can be used many ways in decorating. A bold pattern will emphasize the area it is used on, create a colorful center of interest.

Far wall in this kitchen was deliberately emphasized with harlequin patterned wallpaper to set the dining area apart from the rest of kitchen.

Huge diamonds painted on doors add interesting note, tend to disguise doors.

Discriminating use of color plays important yet inexpensive role in kitchen modernization

Colors give a room character. Some colors suggest warmth or coolness; others make a room appear feminine or masculine, restful or animated.

This kitchen takes on a sophisticated air with its combination of blues and greens.

Blue is the predominant color, used on the floor and appliances, while the green was used as an accent.

The open glass shelves provide a perfect place to show off favorite art pieces.

Save those old cabinets

Orange lacquer and blue-green paint turn discarded kitchen cabinets into a handsome divider used between kitchen and dining area. Matchstick blinds close off pass-through. The interior of the shelves and drawers were painted to match lacquered plywood top. For accent, pulls are painted black.

Small pattern wallpaper suggests colonial theme

Small pattern wallpaper adds colonial charm to this kitchen and inspires the use of imaginative accessories.

Decoy is used as a bookend on the desk. A pewter mug becomes a pencil holder and a tea canister is converted into a wastebasket. Mortar bowl is perfect plant holder.

An old chair and piano bench were rescued from the attic and given a coat of paint and new seat cushions.

Budget ideas add charm, convenience to a kitchen

Oriental prints mounted on the sliding cabinet doors provide interesting kitchen decoration. A collection of menus or favorite recipes could be displayed in the same manner.

Stamp hinges like the ones used in stamp albums hold prints on laminated plastic doors. Clear plastic covers the prints; two-piece hollow rivets fasten them to doors. The same idea could be used on storage units in the living room or child's play room.

New pass-through saves time when cleaning up and gives spacious feeling to eating area

The solid wall separating the kitchen and eating area was partially cut away to form a pass-through, give a more open look in this budget-minded kitchen remodeling project.

By using the same wallpaper in the kitchen and in the eating area you get a feeling of spaciousness—the two areas appear to be one big room. This illusion was furthered by installing the same red hard-surface flooring in both rooms.

Repeated use of turquoise and yellow co-ordinate space into one unit

Remodeling does not always mean a costly investment. Only $22.91 was spent on improving the sink wall. Colorful draperies hung from ceiling above wall cabinets provide extra storage for seldom used items.

Perforated hardboard and shelves were added to wall above sink. Counter top was resurfaced with adhesive-backed vinyl wall covering.

BEFORE

AFTER: $33.21 turned the range wall above into the efficient work center pictured at right.

A new base cabinet which represents the major expense was put on casters for working flexibility. Wall cabinet and perforated hardboard add storage and convenience.

Five inches of space to the left of the range were put to good use as a four-slot file for trays.

Fourteen-inch wall cabinets topped with plywood and foam cushions make a bench in the children's corner. The vinyl cushions are slip-covered with acrylic rugs.

Fabric-covered sliding screens with appliqued angels cover windows. See "how-to" on the next page. Starburst light fixtures follow the "heavenly" theme.

Plan for easy maintenance when you decorate your kitchen-family room

The popular trend toward a combined family room and kitchen poses the problem of how to decorate it so that the area will be easy to maintain and take lots of living wear and tear.

However, the problem is really a simple one with today's washable wallpaper and paint, durable hard surface floor coverings and ceramic tile.

Choose from a wide selection of natural finish wood cabinets that won't show fingerprints or colored metal cabinets that wipe clean in a wink.

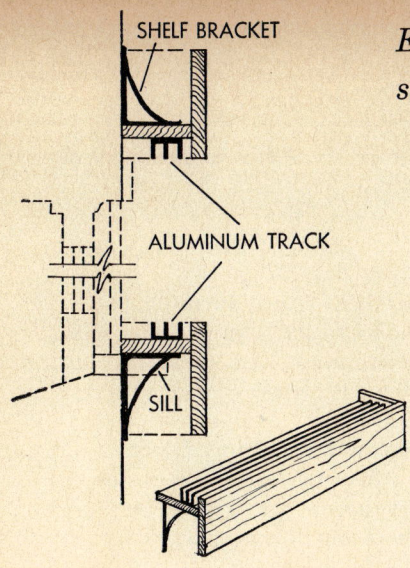

Easy-to-install panels glide smoothly on aluminum track

Wood valance supports and conceals the aluminum sliding track for the hardboard and fabric-covered panels.

To install: Set the upper track support on window trim; level and secure with shelf brackets. Rest lower frame on the window sill; attach as shown in drawing.

Cut the hardboard to allow enough room for panels to be inserted in the track.

Applique winsome angel-dolls on fabric panel covers

A yarn halo slip-stitched to fabric tops this merry angel face. Painted eyes and terry-cloth hair complete features.

The three angels require ½ yard of each fabric shown.

Plaid-bonnet angel wears embroidery grin. Cut clothes from gay prints. Trim with ruffle.

Add a jump rope of yarn tacked to her hand. It loops down when screen is open.

Saucy red-headed angel skips rope of colored yarn.

Bright plaid petticoat peeks out from flower-print dress. Stitching details the toes. Keep each section a simple shape.

A perky red devil wears white trunks and carries pitchfork appliqued with black thread.

Stitch arm, ear, neckline details in white. For fun, we added a black-eyed daisy tail.

"Sleeve" slips over panel

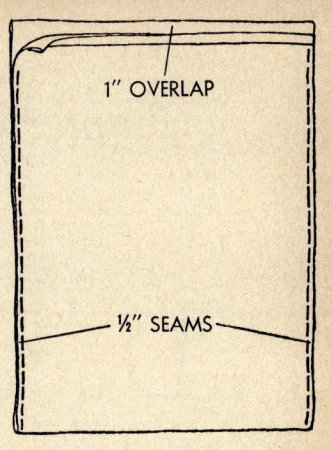

Cut fabric twice the length of panel, plus 2" for top overlap, hems. Allow ½" for side seams.

Stitch ½" roll hem at each end. Apply applique. Fold fabric; let front overlap back as you fit to hardboard. Pin seams.

Stitch side seams so fabric "sleeve" will be taut over panel. Trim, turn, press and slip over the panel.

Pull fabric taut, lap front over back. Pin. Mark line for fastener tape below level of track.

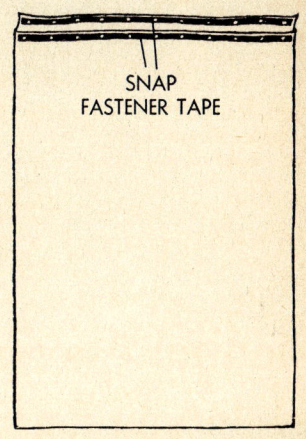

Remove fabric from panel; topstitch tape to fabric. Press; slip over panel. Clip on "U-shape" metal channel top, bottom.

Smooth-sliding channels are available at hardware stores. A top clip fabric guard is optional.

Chapter eight

Decorating ideas for *family rooms*

That it be a carefree place for all of your family... this is the most important qualification of the family room... a room where there's no worry over delicate fabrics or fragile furniture. Use sturdy furnishings so that all can have fun without work.

Here are some ideas to adapt:

1. Plan easy-maintenance materials; wash-and-hang curtains; spot and stain-resistant upholstery fabrics; wipe-up flooring, easy-wash walls.

2. If you have small children, make two sets of slip covers; keep them going in the wash.

3. When furniture is often shifted to accommodate parties or play, ceiling fixtures can be more convenient, safer with children than table lamps with trailing cords.

4. Be sure there's over-all light for television, to avoid eyestrain.

In open-area homes, relate family room furnishings to other areas

Sleekly Contemporary like the living room it adjoins, the family room below uses materials that can take it. Carpeting rejects stains; furniture wipes off; plastic upholstery, counter and table tops resist heat, mars, spots.

Shades of blue, green, rose, and lavender set a color theme executed in nostalgic style combined with contemporary comfort

The antique lighting fixture over the dining table here sets the period theme, is supplemented with additional lights . . . a fluorescent fixture in the ceiling of the bay glimpsed at right, spotlight fixture above the rocker for sewing or reading.

The painted furniture and bright washable pillows echo the gay colors of place mats, china, napkins, and antique glasses. Decorative plates on the high mantel come down for use at parties.

See what you can do with salvaged furniture from the attic or secondhand store! Handy-man abilities are all it takes.

Paint a set of old dining room chairs in gay colors, slip-cover the seats with plastic over foam for comfort. Cut down a dining room table to new dining-coffee table height, refinish it to go with other woods.

There's treasure in the attic — don't let it go to waste. Here, an old-fashioned washstand became a useful record cabinet. Towel rack and legs were removed, a box base added. Paint, new hardware, top covering of adhesive-backed plastic complete the rejuvenation project.

Furnish the family room for teen-age play

Here's a room designed for everyday family use, teen-age parties, too. Round table and captain's chairs serve for family meals, games; chairs join sofa grouping for company.

Pull-down ceiling fixtures are used instead of table lamps, to keep room arrangement flexible. They're supplemented with fluorescent fixtures in window cornices and range hood to light working surfaces. Exhaust fan in hood pulls cooking odors out, keeps family room fresh. Light coffee table is easily moved, rugs roll out of the way for dances.

Ceiling fixtures give plenty of on-the-floor lighting for crawling youngsters, spot decorating, too

Let's face it—at this age, young wrigglers are on the floor most of the time. The long fluorescent fixture in the ceiling gives plenty of over-all light for games, is supplemented by the spot over the television set. Table lamp serves the grown-up reading area, and is safely out of the way of children's quick movements.

Bookshelves line up with the top of the window, further the horizontal look, are high enough so youngsters can't get at them, but convenient for adults. Hard-surface flooring is practical, easy to keep clean.

They will bring all their friends home when you furnish a giddy, gay club room for exclusive teen-age use

Give them a club room of their very own—and you'll find it a center for the neighborhood.

Here, a long valance fixture washes a wall with light, spots a conversation paper that sets the party mood, and also suggests the color theme. Cheering-section bench stores records, games. Hard-surface floor takes rugged use.

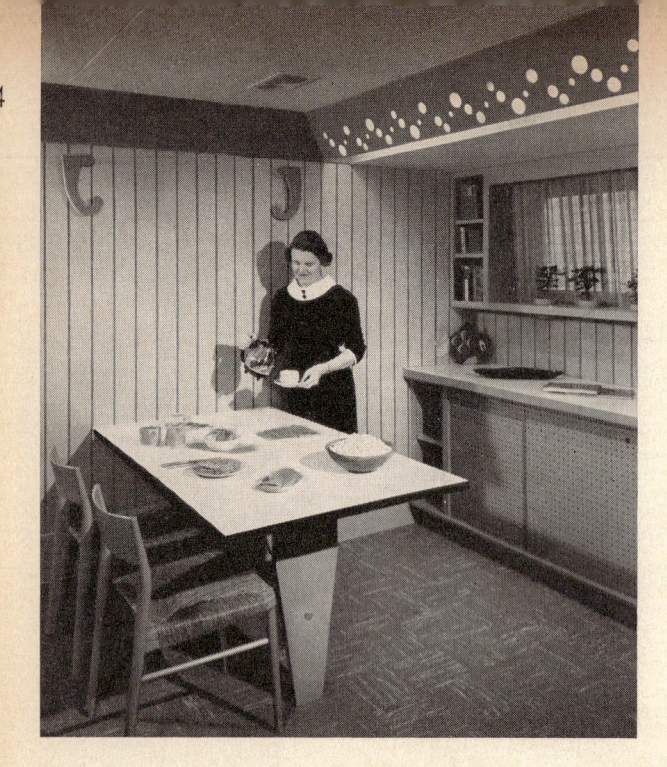

Use your handy-man ingenuity to create a family room

Pipes and ducts, plus lack of natural light, are basement remodeling problems. Here, one solution handles them all—a deep trough running the full length of the room hides pipes, carries fluorescent fixtures for general lighting. Polka-dot cutouts make interesting light patterns, repeat soffit decoration shown below.

Bright color, plenty of light make a basement a cheery center for all family activities

Pull the clown's nose, down drops a plastic-topped table. Near-by strip sockets for appliances let you cook, serve, without running up stairs. Perforated hardboard panels are landing strip for finished model planes, posters from family travels. Acoustic tile ceiling soaks up noise.

Talent can take the place of money to give a home an individual look

They did it themselves—from the actual construction to the decorating. Prefinished wood paneling covers the fireplace wall, its grain enhanced by the soaring piece of driftwood.

A standard rug was cut in a graceful curve, leaving space in front of the hearth to catch stray sparks. Good-looking fire tools were home designed and made. The foam rubber pad gives extra seating.

Pin-up board wall to delight the youngsters

It's a room for family dining, for hobbies, for projects, for playtime fun . . . an all-purpose room that's the heart of the home.

Broad stripes of draperies over the picture window could be made by tacking or snapping panels of different colored ready-mades together. They come apart easily for washing or cleaning.

Dress up chests for attractive storage in the family room

A chest converts to a hi-fi cabinet when you replace the front with a bamboo blind. Home artistry ran bright yarn through the blind in a contemporary striped pattern. Tacked to a pull-out frame, the front comes off for hi-fi repairs.

Oversize whimsical pictures were cut from travel posters. Yours could reflect trips you've taken with the family . . . maps of places you've been, or scenes from cities you loved. Or make pictures from same yarns used on blinds.

Plan family room arrangement so furniture can be easily moved for parties and dancing

Windows that didn't quite come to the floor and an off-center radiator dictated this practical storage and seating unit. It could be built in, or assembled from a variety of sizes of ready-made or unfinished cabinets and chests. Expanded metal, fabric, or bamboo blinds could hide hi-fi speaker and air conditioner as well as a badly placed radiator.

Storage on the wall, a minimum of light furniture out in the room, ceiling spots instead of lamps, give great flexibility for parties. Fluorescent fixtures beneath top shelf would add to over-all light, spot wall decorations.

Color and dual-purpose furnishings convert attic space into combination hobby, guest room

Need space to spread a hobby out, work on it when you will, leave it for a while? Find a spot like this attic room that can be yours most of the time, convert for overnight guests.

Chimney brick here was left exposed to carry out the Early American theme. Daybed serves for guests; chest holds painting and sewing materials, bed linens . . . has a drawer left empty for company belongings. Bamboo blinds painted to match walls conceal tiny windows, give effect of unbroken wall.

Good family room planning includes provision for all hobby interests

Individual shades for narrow windows let you use 39-inch decorator fabric without piecing. With patterned shades like this, it's wise to use a second plain shade next to the glass, so windows look like others in house from outside.

Opaque white fabric on the second set could be used for home movie screen.

Color of rattan and white furniture repeats gold and white wallpaper pattern.

Set color theme with a paper mural

Design an abstract wall mural from construction paper cutouts. Try out on the wall with masking tape before pasting in place. Frame with inexpensive builder's molding.

Design built-ins that can be moved

Attach a panel of painted ¾-inch plywood, cut to fit between moldings. Install full-length metal strips; use adjustable brackets to hold shelves. Panel could also hide electric cord for pin-up or wall light fixture.

Seating is planned for comfort and flexibility in a family room

Individual seats line up to form a handsome sofa, or lift out of their frames easily and move to the floor for informal comfort. Other chairs are light, easy to shift.

Floor-to-ceiling pole of ceramic "beads" is handsome, novel. Patterned rug and hard-surface flooring supply color, form.

Divide basement space into hobby, service, and family room areas

Shuffleboard insets in floor can be bought ready-cut, are easy to install when floor's laid. Perforated hardboard wall is a good place to store game equipment, show off art. In hobby room, tools are hung on a panel on casters — it hides the furnace, can be drawn up closer to workbench when work's in process.

Chapter nine

Decorating ideas for
children's rooms

If your children are past the toddler stage, with definite likes and dislikes, let them help to plan the decorating for their rooms. If you keep the basics simple, you can give them cowboy and Indian trimmings . . . change to something more sophisticated later on. Ideas to think about:
1. If the room is narrow, consider printed vinyl floor covering that comes in 9- or 12-foot widths, doesn't have to be cemented down, gives a quick, inexpensive change.
2. Plan a bed for an overnight guest . . . slumber parties are fun.
3. Arrange play space that will grow into teen-age work space; table tops for finger paints can be converted to homework desks.
4. Consider painted furniture for the growing years. It's easy to change as the child matures.

All set to grow . . . this wall-hung furniture is convenient from nursery to college. Use unfinished pieces, or make your own. Any piece can be lowered or raised in seconds.

Fasten metal standards to wall, slip screws on back of furniture into keyholes in strips. Colors can change as child grows, for quick and inexpensive redecorating.

Brilliant color sets a military theme in a bedroom for a growing boy

Pick a wallpaper that sets the military theme—be sure it's washable, like the cotton carpet, cotton-ticking draperies, rugged spread. Finish storage units and desk to suit room.

Pack rooms with color to please a child

Convert an old chest to a special baby dresser. Remove top drawer front, add hinges, install a magnetic lock that lets you open and close it even while holding Baby.

Paint inside a gay color, stock it with nursery needs. Later on, chest can become a study desk.

BEFORE

Circus theme doesn't quite come off, is dulled by dark rug, plain draperies. Spreads are awkward length, chest is a touch too tall to go beneath the window.

AFTER

Striped draperies, dust ruffles, headboards give a finished look. Corners of bedspreads were cut, boxed in, tailored. Legs of chest were removed . . . now it fits under window. Gay rug was added.

113

Make simple, handy wall racks for favorite books, toys, and records

Nail wood strips to small wood blocks, then screw to wall studs. Quarter-round molding holds books on shelf. Other ideas:

1. Set the color theme with a medley of color in floor tiles; pick up one color for walls, another for curtains, another for spreads and the fabric on the chair.

For a change, choose colors from tile that you haven't used.

2. Use pull-down light fixture instead of easily tipped floor or table lamps; prevent accidents.

Every little girl likes the "fairy princess" look at the dress-up age

Top tier of curtains hides wall above window, middle and lower tiers open with separate traverse cords. It's easier for child to operate if cords are on pulleys ... avoids tangles.

Salute a child's hobbies through room decor

Model airplanes fly above a boy's desk in a light and airy suite that was once a dingy attic corner.

Blue paint unites a built-in desk, woodwork and folding storage doors which save floor space by folding instead of swinging out.

Touches of red used as accent in study area might be repeated for rug, spreads of adjoining bedroom.

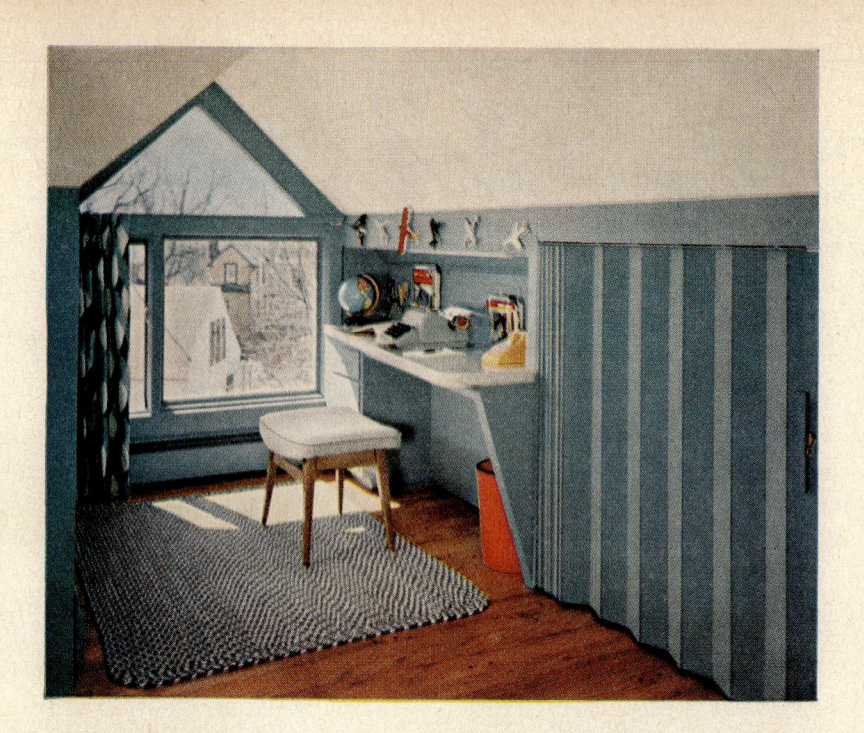

A map for fun and learning

Copy a map to scale on graph paper, transfer to perforated hardboard.

Cut out with a jigsaw; paint and mount on wall with furring strips.

Thumbtacks or tiny flags might mark countries studied in school.

Spotlight treasures with a pole lamp

Good for a child's room because it fits tight against ceiling and floor, won't tip, a pole lamp gives good reading light for the bed, spots a young girl's collection of toys. It takes up little space, is easily moved when furniture arrangement changes as the child grows up.

Perforated hardboard above the bed holds added treasures, is painted to match the shelves, blend with the bedspread. Low chair is just the right height for putting on shoes.

Teach him to find his own clothes

A little homemade art work helps you teach a youngster to find his own clothes in the morning, dresses up his room at the same time.

Unfinished chest painted to blend with bright draperies or spreads is decorated with pasted-on cutouts or painted outlines of socks, handkerchiefs, sweaters, underwear, outer clothing.

A freestanding storage wall divides one big room into two

It used to be one big room shared by two youngsters. Now each has his own room. In between is an ingenious storage wall of 2x4s, covered with perforated hardboard. Play counter becomes two private desks when folding door is pulled across.

Cubbyholes above store treasures, cabinet below holds more toys. In future it could store a portable typewriter. Bench pushes out of the way under the desk.

Make a dado of fabric to match pillows and draperies

Fabric that resembles Spanish tiles harmonizes with a collection of bullfight pictures. It's used as wall covering as well as for pillows, draperies.

When cutting fabric to be used as wall covering, make sure of the pattern match as you cut each strip.

Apply wallpaper paste *to wall* rather than to the fabric. Smooth each strip of fabric on wall, making sure edges stick.

As you finish hanging each strip, wipe off paste spots at once with a damp cloth.

Rooms to grow in — decorated with fun and fancy

Pink's popular—and it needn't be wishy-washy. Start with crisply colored print. Concentrate pattern on big areas such as the curtains and spread.

Select the solid tones for the tester ruffle, canopy and blanket. Spark with a contrasting note in painted furniture.

Make a matching bed for a favorite doll. Scrap of pattern is spread; washcloth is blanket.

Picture is based on a motif from spread plus scrapbasket pieces

Start with pattern cut from fabric used in a child's room. Sew to felt or window shade; add more bits of bright fabric. Run painted dowels or brass rods through top and bottom to hang.

Here, a happy clown from the bedspread inspired a hanging where he holds a clutch of gay balloons. You might "paint" a sewing machine picture with flowers, boats, horses, if your child doesn't happen to be a circus fan.

A delightful shadow box shows off all her cherished collection

Real shingles on the roof, scalloped shelves and eaves give a story-book air. Boards can be bought already scalloped at lumber dealer, or done at home from a paper pattern.

Unit needn't be deep—six-inch shelf is ample for most toys. Or, vary the idea by omitting shelves. Instead, cut a backing of perforated hardboard and hang toys from hooks. Under the bottom scallop, mount a fluorescent fixture.

Same pattern, two colors divide sleeping areas

One long room shared by two boys is given visual separation by using the same fabric in two different colors, to define each boy's section of the room. The sturdy cotton material is even used to cover the doors of the freestanding wardrobe.

The areas are still further separated by means of a bamboo blind, hung on an overhead track so it pulls across the room.

Scroll headboard is painted

Nicely feminine, what looks like a fashionable wrought-iron bedstead is really just a design painted on the wall. Draw design on wrapping paper; transfer to wall.

A wooden shelf, held to the wall with brackets, carries a decorative ruffle.

Try new furniture with young ideas

Matching storage units serve a child at two ages. Take legs off one, stack for baby clothes—easier for Mother.

Later on, replace legs, set units side by side so toddler can reach into them. Bench is good place to rest toys, and right height for putting on shoes.

Stack units are infinitely flexible. Storage-drawers fit on top of each other, rest on long bench. Pad and toss pillows make it a sofa.

Same drawers and bench could be rearranged for television, record-player, and record storage when the child becomes a teen-ager.

Hideaway storage, one-color scheme, give the impression of space in a small room

A little space was stolen from a closet in an adjoining room to take care of storage drawers that pull out of the headboard, more drawers that serve as bedside tables, extend into closet.

Vertical siding accentuates ceiling height, as does the wall trim inspired by the flooring motif. Shades of pink are the only colors used, showing how dramatic a two-tone scheme can be.

Tasseled bedspread is in keeping with the very feminine room scheme.

A storage headboard is both a ladder and a shelf piece for little boy treasures

Just as much fun as the jungle gym outside, and sturdy enough to take lots of climbing, this ladder and shelf bunk bed will suit young boys. If there's only one boy in the family, the extra bunk will be ready for his overnight guests.

Mount a wallpaper map or a series of other maps on sliding closet doors. Protect with spray that lets you scrub them, resists fingerprints and soil.

Arrange two beds foot to foot on a long wall, leave space for study in a room designed for the homework set

You'll need a thirteen-foot wall to accommodate two beds foot to foot, but it's a good way to make a study-playroom of an ordinary bedroom.

Around-the-corner valance conceals fluorescent light for reading and study, is repeated at the other end of the room. Wall spots supplement overall light from above.

Boldly patterned rug is in good harmony with shades of orange used for fabrics, walls.

Chapter ten

Decorating ideas for bedrooms

You spend about a third of your life in bed, refreshing yourself from working and playing hours... and your first thought for the bedroom should be comfort, to give you the healthful sleep you need. Pleasant and pretty surroundings contribute to comfort, too, so plan for beauty. Here are some ideas:

1. If you're tall, consider the new king-size mattresses. Linens are available for them, too.
2. You may like the easy care of hard-surface floors. But have a soft, warm rug to step on when you get out of bed.
3. Plan window treatments for both privacy and view—that let you black out the room for sleeping comfort. Consider opaque shades, venetian blinds with slats that overlap, lock out light.
4. Look for chests with drawers that fit shirts; cabinets with places for purses; shallow drawers for sweaters and lingerie.
5. Plan for easy care—fitted sheets, drip-dry sheets and cases; blankets from man-made fibers that wash, tumble dry; rugs that can be laundered.

Here's help for bedroom planning to insure comfort and beauty

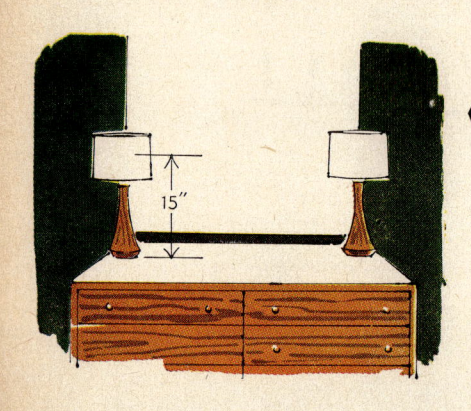

Good light on you

An average dressing table 30 inches high requires a lamp that measures 15 inches from table top to shade center.

A 36-inch dresser should be equipped with lamps that measure 22 inches from dresser top to center of shade.

If you use white translucent shades, there will be no color distortion for make-up.

Make a floor plan

It's important to know all room dimensions when shopping for furniture, rugs, curtains, and so on. Take a floor plan with you—one that gives exact measurements. Show height of windows from floor, so you can choose chests to go under them.

Show sizes and heights of pieces you'll keep, so you can select lamps, mirrors.

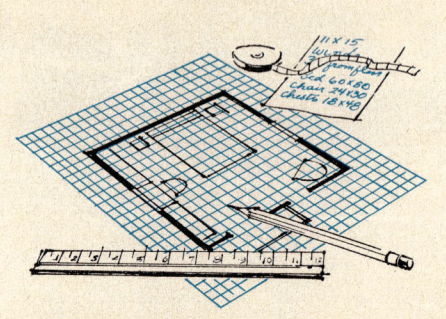

Add sitting area

If your bedroom is big enough, let room do double duty as an adult family room or study; a place to read, relax, write letters.

Add an easy chair or two, a desk. Provide over-all general light to counteract glare of specific light you'll use for reading, working, sewing, or from television.

Use every precious inch of bedroom space . . . select storage that fits . . . vibrant colors that say "good morning"

Here's a happy blending of old design, new comfort. A true Colonial half-tester covers 20th Century twin beds. Spreads of Early American inspiration are topped by modern foam bolsters. Apothecary chests become bedside stands that add to storage space.

You might copy the country look by using a brick pattern instead of planking for the wall. It comes in three-dimensional plastic or in wallpaper.

You can split a big bedroom into dressing,

A spacious bedroom in an older home can look young again with a fresh color scheme. This rejuvenation project began with a ready-made spread and a slip cover for the chaise longue. The rug's old, but paint's new. Outdated lamps have been replaced with new ones, inches taller.

To ease a one-bath-to-serve-the-whole-family problem, twin basins and storage were added, screened from the rest of the room with louvered panels attached to the bed.

sleeping, and sitting areas

Change your color scheme... rearrange the furniture for better use... here are seven ideas for you to adapt

1. Louvered screen used as room divider permits circulation of air, gives privacy to basin area. Height of curved tester also helps to hide the dressing area from view.
2. Even though bedside lamps stand away from a wall, there are no tangled cords to trip over. Outlets are installed in floor. Plan furniture arrangement carefully before cutting carpet for electric outlets.
3. New bolster pillow is same width as the bed, makes spread look neat. Tubular cases with a hemmed border at either end are available.
4. Sliding closet doors come faced with full-length mirrors.
5. Strong pattern is used sparingly. White in the mass of curtains, dust ruffle, screen, lamp shades, painted desk chair, softens brilliance.
6. Tall lamps replace older, shorter ones, are right height for reading.
7. New mattress and springs were selected to suit weight of occupants. Both foam and innerspring types come in several different styles.

Gain a new dressing room most economically, without window changes, keeping the carpentry simple. Linoleum floor blending with carpet color might be used in basin area.

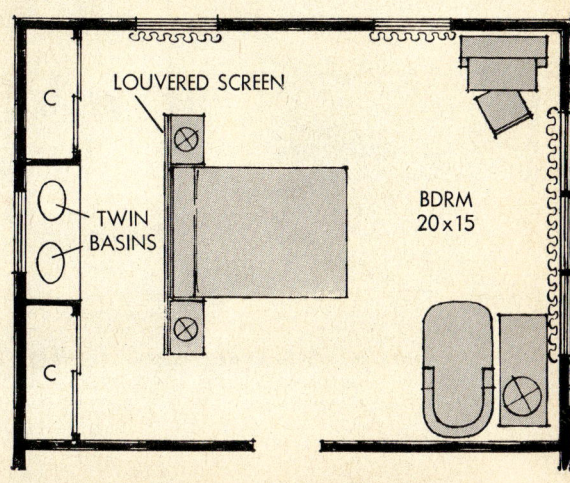

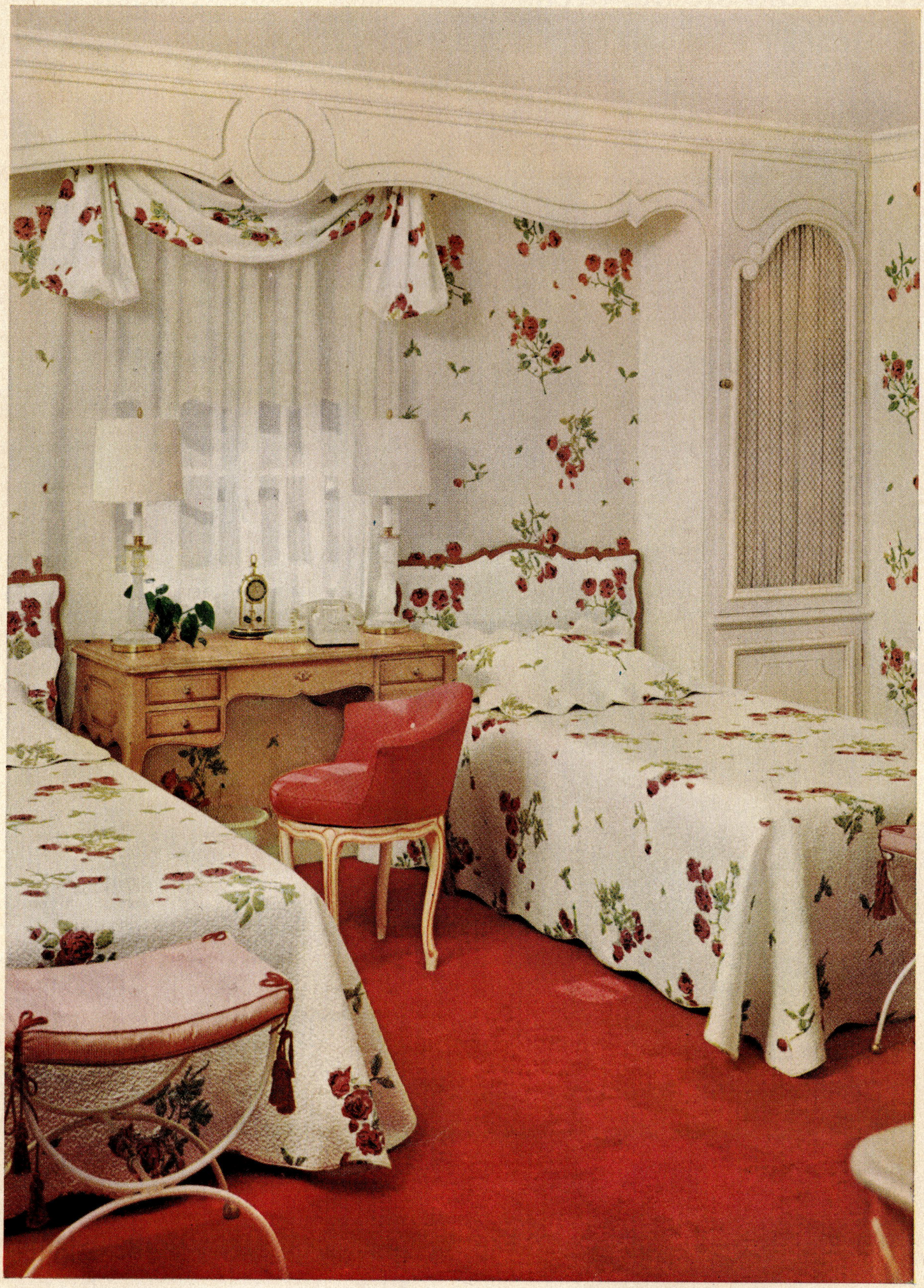

Fabric patterns set an elegant theme

← If you have a long wall with a window centered on it, here's a good arrangement. Make a bed niche by building narrow, ceiling-high closets at each side; run a decorative cornice across the wall. Upholster headboards, make spreads and window swag of the same patterned fabric; use matching wallpaper.

Desk instead of two night tables is an excellent choice . . . it fits the space perfectly, has dual use. Cornice lighting would be good here, to supplement the bedside lamps. Spreads have scalloped tops that fold to enclose pillows, add decorative note. Carpet, upholstery, are a cheery tone from fabric pattern.

Adapt one of these six budget ideas

1. Heavy gold brocade spread lights up a room with neutral walls, dark floor. Yours could be of inexpensive cotton. 2. Bolster pillow has tailored look . . . linens are available for them. 3. Hatboxes—leather here—are unusual, practical storage. Yours could be wicker. 4. Long bench could also serve as suitcase rack, slipper seat. Make yours of plywood with legs you can buy. 5. Bookcases used as bedside tables keep reading matter at hand. 6. Prints could be unframed, mounted on hardboard, or in ready-made frames.

↓

Choose furniture that makes the most of every inch of space

Hang as much of the furniture on the walls as you can. It makes cleaning easier and gains valuable floor space. Lamps hang, too, and so does the yellow wall-model telephone.

Space-making furniture designs include the hanging vanity, the wall panel above the bed, long narrow bench that holds both a storage chest and a television set.

Window shades are installed from the bottom to give privacy for dressing while still admitting light.

Ceiling high accordion doors come ready to install, can partition an alcove, go across an entire wall.

Wall light fixture over the storage chest gives needed glow to counteract television glare. Long tube light at dressing table keeps shadows away from chin, make-up goes on easier.

From the stained floor planks to the linens and bright walls, color scheme perks up a dark room, says a cheery "good morning."

If you're moving, or like variety, here's change-about furniture

← Furniture that shifts arrangement easily, plus a portable color scheme, lets you spark up drab walls, give a rented home personality. Often you're not permitted to paint or paper or drive nails in the wall — or you may not want to invest the money and labor in someone else's property when your stay will be temporary.

The chests stack on top of each other, fit tightly together at the sides. The desk can turn the corner or fit flat against the wall, depending on the space. The head panels have hook-on shelves, separate freestanding night tables. The mirror and the bulletin board attach to your furniture instead of to the wall.

For a portable color scheme, choose plain fabrics, use blending tones in every room, so you can switch them to fit changed dimensions in the next house. Instead of one or two big rugs, you might choose several small ones that can be taped together in different shapes, make a fresh pattern when you move.

Small rooms need space savers

One fairly massive piece of furniture that really fits the space often makes a room seem bigger than an assortment of smaller ones.

One long wall is all it takes for this stunning half tester arrangement over twin beds. Ruffle and curtains are hung from a frame made of strips of wood, fastened to the ceiling with screws or bolts.

White lining of curtains is a deliberate color accent . . . sometimes both sides are of a pattern. Ball fringe trims both curtain and ready-made spread. Dado is oftenest used in dining rooms, but was frequently found in Colonial bedrooms.

Fluorescent fixture under canopy would supplement bedside lamps, partially hidden by draperies.

Splurge on some new pieces; economize by renovating others to fit into scheme

A beautiful new bed, lamp tables and benches made it necessary to economize on other pieces.

Old dressers were covered with paper used on the walls . . . sprayed for protection. A glass top prevents soiling the surface. Bright scheme makes a dark room more cheery.

Gain both storage and space with a corner closet, compact furniture

Small room—inadequate storage? For a bigger look, better hideaway space, build a closet into the corner.

Headboard has sliding doors to hide bedside clutter, a shelf above for radio, clock and snacks. Matching footlocker holds bedding; serves as a seat or luggage rack.

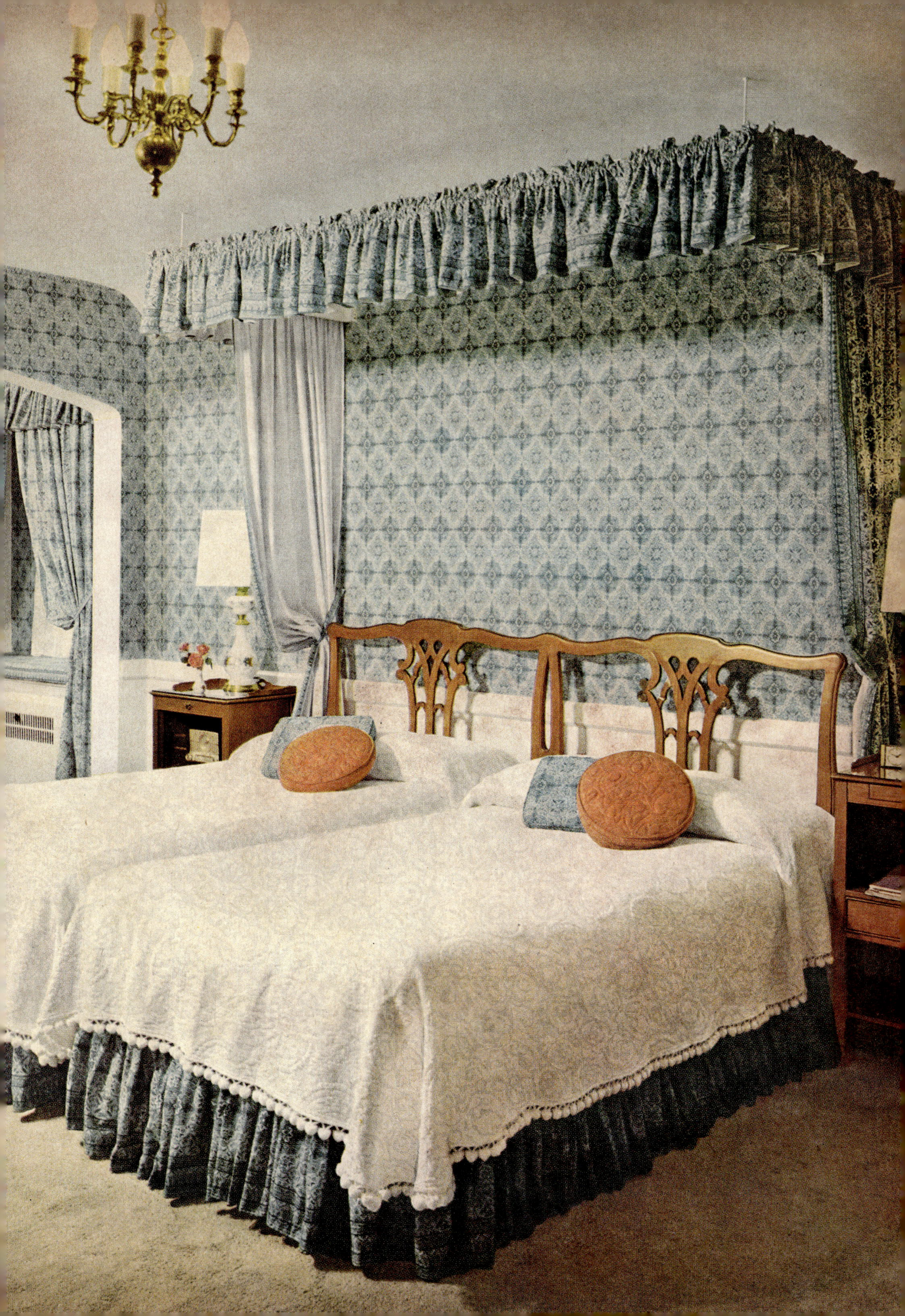

Chapter eleven

Decorating ideas for bathrooms

Even in the tiny space of the average bathroom, something distinctive can be achieved in decorating. Relate bath colors to those of the room it opens on . . . whether hall or bedroom. Using master plan colors relates it to whole house. Other ideas for bathroom decorating:

1. Fixture color is a major part of the scheme. Repeat it elsewhere . . . in a stripe, in the shower curtain, rug, towels.
2. You get lots of luxury at little price with wall-to-wall carpeting. First, make a paper pattern, cutting out spaces for fixtures. Trace pattern to back of rug. Be sure to invert pattern—use knife to cut. Rug needn't be bound.
3. If there's a window over the tub, install a second shower rod and curtain. It keeps the sill dry, looks pretty, too.
4. If fixture color doesn't "go" with the general color scheme, tie it in by using one of the master plan colors in strength, another as accent. Combine both with fixture color in a pattern, in window or shower curtains, or paper.

Plan your bathroom decorating to blend with the over-all color scheme of your home

If several share a single bath, consider the usefulness of a double sink. There are compact ones that take less space than you'd think.

Where Father shaves, arrange mirror lighting to extend far enough down so lower chin isn't shadowed. Always have truthful light in the bath, rather than a flattering glow. And select the colors you use in it under the same light as you have in your bath.

You can change the color scheme quickly and often if bath fixtures are white or neutral. Several sets of towels and shower curtains in different colors will do the trick. Change often, but always include some of color that matches or blends with fixtures.

Because there's always steam in a bathroom, it's important to select fabrics that stay crisp when damp, won't shrink or stretch, will wash easily.

Use same colors for bed and bath

Cool, clear blues and fresh greens are repeated, over and over, with more green in the partial bath than in the bedroom.

They appear in forget-me-not pattern of linens; in solid blue of bath wall and in bed trappings to unite the two areas.

Lots of bathroom storage space means fewer steps

Louvered doors cover cabinets that store week's supply of towels, other bath accessories. Shallow drawers hold everyday needs.

Washable wall covering in bronze, gold, white, sets the color theme. Antique picture frame borders mirror. Marble counter could be copied in plastic.

← *Antique accessories can give charm to a modern bath*

A Contemporary lavatory-vanity combination in the bath is fitted with chair, mirror frame and towel rack to blend in style with the Early American feeling of the bedroom.

Warm gold gives cool green a cheerful look.

The green of the rug and antique gold of the spread are repeated in some of the bath towels. As harmonious accents, orange and brown towels are added.

Pretty patterned bed linens can also co-ordinate style and color. Here, an interesting Pennsylvania Dutch motif is featured.

Feature bright color in a bath for the children

Wood walls in bedroom and bath are brightened with a generous dash of vivid red in sturdy spreads, gay towels. Change colors as young tastes grow sophisticated.

Good ideas: twin lavatories, plastic wastebasket, clock. Roll-type towel at lavatory side snaps together at ends; can be reached but not pulled down.

←

Gain full family use with a compartmented bathroom

Young family — big old bathroom? Turn it into three sections, two with stools, lavatories, one with tub, shower. Plastic ceiling conceals fluorescent fixtures, gives good light for shaving, make-up.

Sliding doors in bath section are ceiling-high, make remodeling easier. Colors are accents used elsewhere in the house.

Use color and pattern to furnish a bath so it will be both pretty and practical

If you're blessed with a bath of ample proportions, here's an ingenious way to use that bonus space in a manner both functional and decorative.

Open storage shelves and a hatrack of metal and glass weren't actually designed for bathroom use, but they certainly adapt well. The shelf unit becomes a room divider and storage-display case for your most beautiful towels. Painted chair with rush seat adds after-the-bath dressing convenience, advances stylish black accent.

Fleur de lis ... French ... formal— classic wallpaper design sets the color and decor of this guest powder room

Even the tiniest space can take on period enchantment. This one was transformed with a fleur-de-lis wallpaper pattern in white and gold, sprayed for protection against water spots. An antique picture frame holds the mirror; light fixtures have crystal drops; ornate fixtures add a touch of luxury.

Sink cabinets hold a supply of guest linens, and shallow drawers take the place of a medicine cabinet. A good window treatment for this room would be a white Austrian shade, with no curtains.

Matching paper and fabric interpret the style in a Provincial bathroom

Minimize the visual break of windows by curtaining them in a fabric to match wallpaper pattern.

You'll be able to choose from many—some documentary like this one, some featuring designs that reflect your family hobbies, such as dogs or horses, sailing or fishing.

An old marble-topped washstand serves as a dressing table, antique china as accessories, right down to the wastebasket.

Supplement wall-lights at sink with an antique pull-down fixture, or a modern copy of one, over the dressing table area.

Adapt one of these decorating ideas to your own period scheme for a bathroom

1. Decorative tile counter has Early American motif, cleans easily along with splashboard.
2. Storage units of knotty pine with hammered iron hardware, carry out the furnishings style of the house.
3. Drawers under the sink hold bottles, toothpaste, make-up, take the place of a too-modern looking medicine cabinet.
4. Towels are conveniently placed for both sink and tub.
5. Apothecary bottles on the counter add to Early American feeling, are practical containers for soap flakes, scouring powder, bath oils—or what you will.
6. Antique light fixtures flank the mirror, supplement more modern fluorescents overhead.

Decorator touches that make a bath gay, feminine or tailored needn't be costly

←

You can dress up any bathroom for youngsters without making a major remodeling change. Jolly clown rug on the floor goes into the washing machine, fluffs dry. Shower curtain, towels are the red-red that very young children always like best.

Stool painted to match lets smallest ones climb up to wash their own hands, get a drink without bothering mother. It's a good spot for finger painting, other splashy fun with toys that take to the water.

Practical plastics dress up an elegant half-bath that doubles as a powder room for guests

Plastic-finished paper sets a sophisticated theme. Vanity counter is surfaced with same vinyl that covers floor. Chair cushion is lush velvet treated to withstand soil, spots. Other ideas:

1. Decorative grille is made from dowels and wood balls, painted.
2. Plug-in valance lighting has two tubes—one is up-light that lights entire wall, other is down-light for primping.
3. Wall-to-wall mirror doubles apparent size of room, makes it light, airy.

137

Inexpensive materials produce a light, modern bath

BEFORE: The room always looked messy, with no place to hide clutter. Inadequate light bounced off mirror, caused glare. The floor was badly cracked. Window looked right into upstairs room of a neighbor.

AFTER: What a difference imaginative use of some ready-mades has achieved. Commercial lavatory, cabinet, medicine chest have modern lines, were easily installed without expensive plumbing relocation.
  Sheet plastic was framed to make light-diffusing divider and window shutter. Divider was framed with wood, shutter with handy-man aluminum. Swing-out units above the lavatory hide medicine chest items. The splashboard and top of the vanity are of flexible plastic. Valance made from perforated hardboard carries fluorescents across room.

Remodel old bathrooms to get maximum use, new beauty

BEFORE: Cut-up wall surface made room look smaller. Window was hard to waterproof for new shower. Crevices were hard to clean.

AFTER: 1. Small ventilator-fan serves for air circulation, replaces window. 2. Laminated-plastic wall covering is waterproof, wipes clean. Standard 2½x5-foot sheets are used on the wall; pieces for lavatory and splash areas cut to size. 3. New suspended ceiling is lighted from above with two fluorescent fixtures. Corrugated fiberglass is removable for access. 4. New shower is adjustable, can be shifted to height of child or adult. 5. Shower curtain is of plastic-backed jersey fabric. 6. Easy-slide hooks are part of the shower rod.

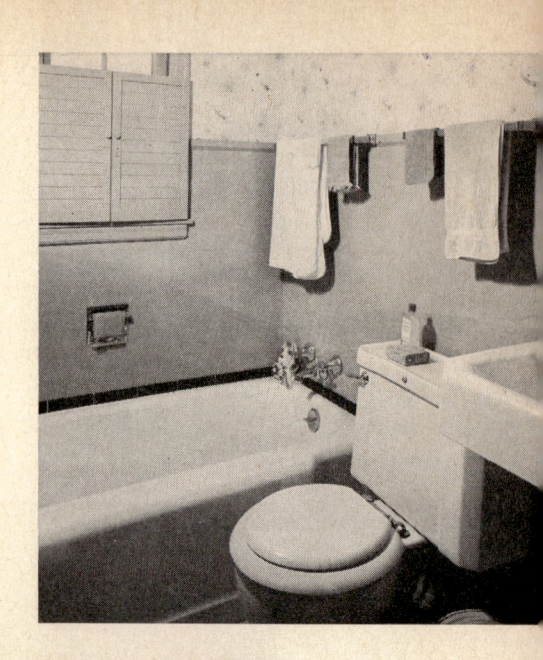

Renovation made room for baby needs, washer-dryer, too

BEFORE: There was no storage, even for minimum baby supplies which had to be carried in each time. Old heater gave uneven warmth. Door was awkwardly placed. Lighting was unattractive and ineffective.

AFTER: 1. Useless door was closed off, provided usable wall space. 2. Kitchen sink, instead of usual lavatory, makes baby bathing easier. 3. Washer-dryer fits under counter. Using old plumbing location saved money. 4. Kitchen-type wall cabinets give good 2-foot-deep storage, come in many finishes. 5. Heat diffuser replaces old heater, circulates furnace heat. 6. New lighting fixtures installed both above and below cabinets are adjustable to bright or indirect light. 7. Shower head has variable spray control, can be adjusted to child or adult height.

Chapter twelve

Decorating ideas for dens and guest rooms

It's nice to have guests, even nicer to make them really comfortable in an inviting room. Den-guest room decorating can be as stylish as for a living room. Here are ideas to make it a success:
1. Since dual-purpose pieces will be used for sitting more than for sleeping, select for sitting comfort everyday, enough sleeping comfort for occasional use.
2. Leave at least six feet of clearance in front of a sofa bed so it can be made up without moving heavy furniture.
3. Provide space for guest suitcases, such as a folding luggage rack. It can be stored between time, or—topped with a tray—become a serving table.
4. Leave some free closet space for guests. Or look for a handsome freestanding wardrobe as part of the furniture.
5. Consider a decorating scheme built around family hobbies—wallpaper with hobby motifs, mementoes, maps of travels; pictures that relate to family interests.
6. Light as you would the living room. But be sure there's a good light for a guest to read by when the bed is made up and he's at ease for the night.

Make sure there is enough storage room for guest linens, family supplies, too

You might find storage space behind a padded sofa-back for guest pillows and blankets. Linens could go in the twin cabinet at the right.

Back is hinged front of storage cabinet, snaps into place with metal catches.

Bed is studio couch that fits under cabinet for sitting comfort, pulls out for sleeping. Tailored spreads are of sturdy material that goes to the wash.

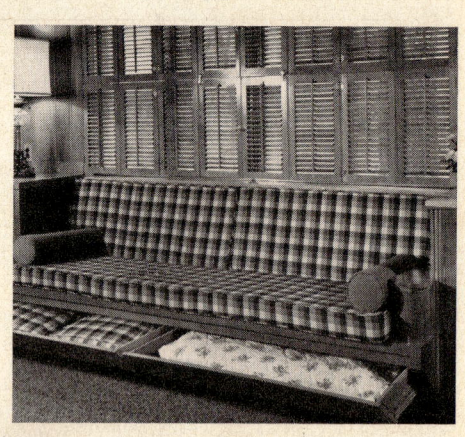

Plan extra uses for the den-guest room. Here, open shelves convert it to a library-study; closed storage hides card tables, stationery, family games, record player, hi-fi.

Use the room for sewing, too. Look for a machine in a cabinet that's a handsome chest or table when closed. Have plenty of good working light.

A handy place for extra storage is in built-in tray drawers beneath a combination sofa-guest bed. Running the full length of the bed, they're deep enough to hold blankets, pillows, plus some linens.

If trays must come out, or if you have a sofa bed that pulls into the room, place only light tables in front of it, so they can be easily moved to make the bed.

Shutters above dress the wall, suit the tailored room treatment.

Bright color, furnishings, lend a living room look to guest room-study

Bright idea where there's no view are these grillwork sliding doors covering a window. They could be of inexpensive expanded metal framed with wood. White sofa is practical with new soil-repellent treatment. Painted chairs are good accent. If you do your own, choose fabric first, paint to blend.

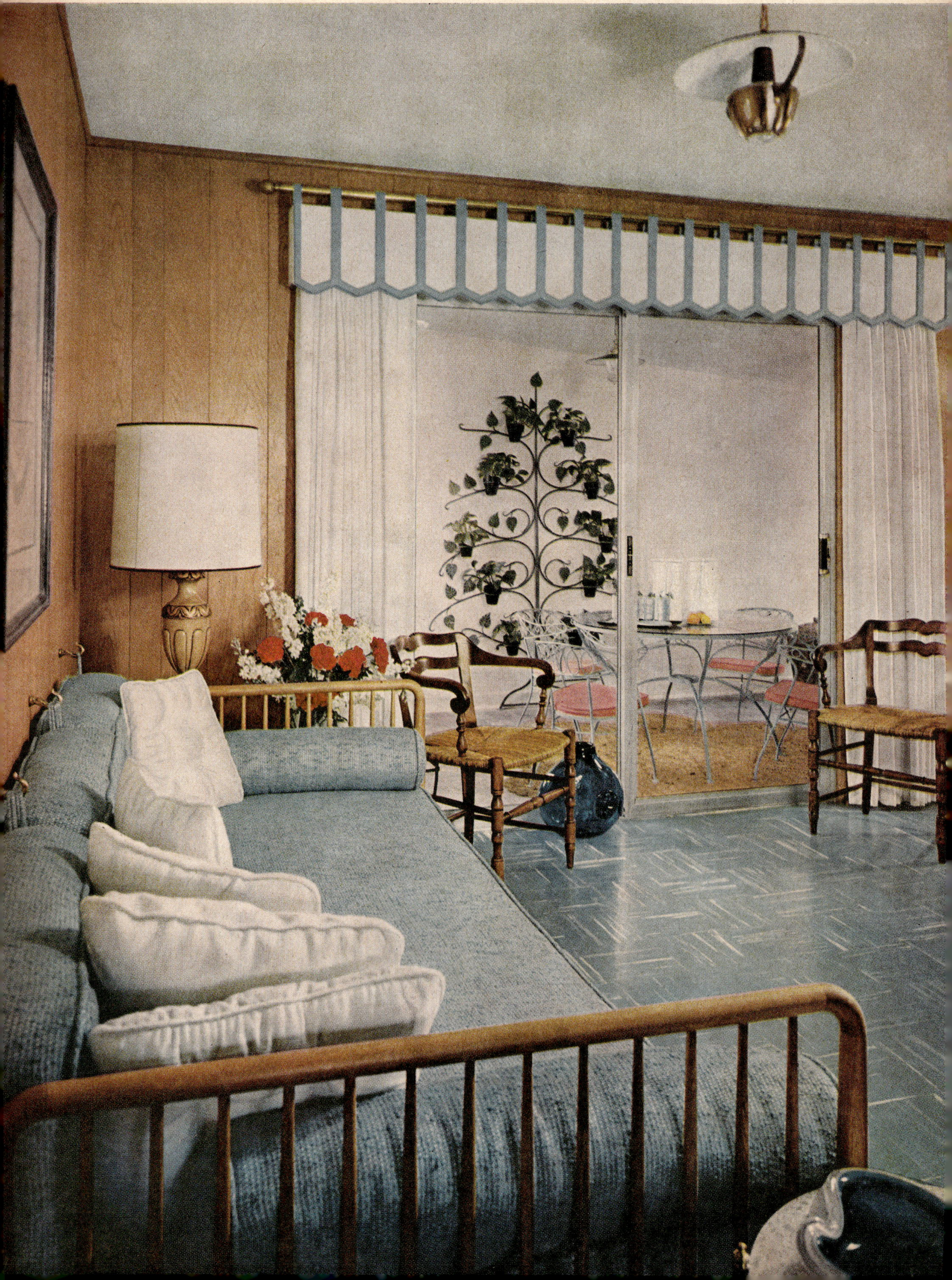

Family rooms accommodate overnight guests

← Practical and pretty, here is a family room that doubles as a guest room, too. The bed is a twin size, with big bolsters hung on the wall to give seating depth. Some new daybeds have an adjustable back frame that shifts from shallow depth for sitting to regulation depth when bed is to be made up for sleeping.

The view onto the covered terrace is framed by draperies that pull for privacy. Cornice is trimmed with heavy tape that extends into tabs for hanging. You could copy the design in felt that needs no hems, is easily worked.

For convenience, provide near-by storage to hold guest linens, clothes and game equipment.

Frame a bed for storage, good looks

This handsome wall of shelves was a handyman project. First, the space was carefully planned and sketched on paper to fit around the sofa bed, making sure that first shelf was high enough to miss heads of seated persons.

Next, shelf backing was lined with marble-patterned paper, shelves fitted. They extend on either side of sofa to form end tables.

Paper is sprayed to make it spot and moisture resistant. Sofa upholstery is plastic.

With dark, nonreflecting walls, you'll need bigger bulbs to get adequate lighting.

↓

Furnishings will let a single room lead a double life

The room pictured at left is an alcove off the living room of an old-fashioned house, turned to good use as guest space and as a quiet sitting room.

Careful planning and measuring were required to get the most from the room. A floor plan was an essential shopping aid when figuring the exact dimensions of the sofa bed and the comfortable armchair and ottoman. They have the appearance of being big, but are actually scaled delicately to fit just such a room as this. Light-colored upholstery adds to the spacious look, as does small checked pattern of the wall covering.

The window wall was made the focal decorating point here, with the window itself shuttered, then framed in a wall-wide series of shelves, stained to match the shutters. Books and treasured family heirlooms are displayed here.

Narrow end table holds a lamp that's good to read by, seated or in bed.

Small scaled sofa beds are a good choice for a living room-guest room

This living room converts quickly to an occasional guest room because the two sofas turn easily into beds. Seats are comfortable mattresses; slanted bolsters come off at night. The small scale of the sofas makes it possible to use a pair in a room of average size.

Guest linens, blankets, pillows store in the chest near the door.

Furniture arrangement uses the room space well, defines traffic lanes. Sofa at left is positioned to gain an entryway; sofa in foreground sits into room to leave space so door can open easily.

Bright chair can be drawn into conversation grouping when needed. Draperies of wall color increase a sense of spaciousness.

Brilliant accent colors give a guest room-den a look of distinction

A dramatic splash of orange enlivens space-making white. Lightweight coffee table moves easily, sofa opens into a bed for two. Wall map is a photographic enlargement hung from brass towel rods. Jog in wall, made important with deep color, forms a striking background for picture.

Color and pattern spruce up a den-guest room

A fabric of Provincial pattern used generously ties together an assortment of furniture of mixed styles, differing wood finishes.

Planned for a single guest, this small room is useful also for reading or sewing. A good substitute for the table at the far end of the bed would be a sewing machine in a table-style cabinet. Dresser could store sewing necessaries, with room also for guest linens and clothing.

Wall lamp of the type that lets you adjust the angle of its beam could serve both for sewing, reading.

Co-ordinate furniture leftovers with a stunning color scheme

Pink and purple color scheme — against a white background — is derived from coin-dot pattern of papered ceiling. Other ideas:

1. Colorful couch covers — here of linen — could be copied in inexpensive denim.
2. Box spring cover and separate throw top conceal made-up bed . . . good treatment when guest will stay for several days.
3. Pillow bolsters could be styled with zipper opening to gain storage for bedding.
4. Shutters come already assembled, in a variety of sizes. All you do is paint or stain to match color scheme.

Start with a distinctive pattern, use it lavishly, repeat around the room to capitalize on its beauty

The scheme began with a large-patterned print used for the draperies on one wall, repeated in big pillows on the beds, and in matching paper on opposite wall. Decorator touch: each valance pleat presents one block of the pattern.
 Dark walls such as these need lots of light. Good place for extra illumination is an under-the-valance trough. Let valance project far enough so draperies won't be damaged.

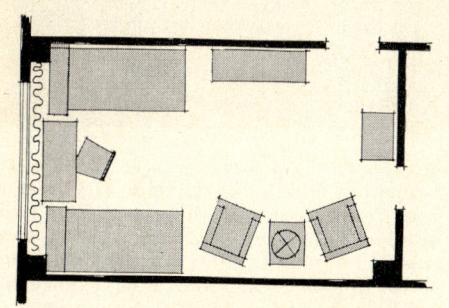

Placement of bookcase headboards and desk permits draperies to hang smoothly. Furniture is arranged so traffic between doors passes by, not through.

Give old furniture a new look with a coat of black paint, hardware that has an Oriental feeling, seems related to pattern of paper and fabric.
 Bright accent color of chair is repeated in rows of small pillows on the beds. The couch covers blend with the color of the carpet, minimize size of beds, help to make the room seem larger.

Furnish a third bedroom to serve as sewing room, guest bedroom, study and family recreation room

Many new homes today have three bedrooms but lack a family room. If you and your family can get along with the two smaller bedrooms, you can convert the master bedroom to an informal gathering place, plus a guest room, plus a place to carry on sewing projects and hobbies.

First and most important is to plan the activities you want the room to serve. Decide on the kind and amount of seating and sleeping space you require, storage needed for all activities. For example if working with ceramic tiles is your hobby, you'll need shallow drawers to store the tiles, hideaway space somewhere for in-work projects. You'll want bookshelves, a drawer or two for guests, closet space to accommodate company clothing.

You'll use the room with greatest pleasure if decorating is simple. Choose colorful materials designed for easy upkeep.

Set up a sewing corner that will double as a writing-study center

Organize your sewing needs into a decorative wall arrangement. A piece of painted plywood is fitted with spindles for colorful threads. Knitting needles tuck into a bright ball of yarn. A big toss pillow hangs convenient as a pincushion. Additional storage for patterns and materials is available in desk drawers.

When you need a desk, just remove the portable sewing machine. Pin-up lamp gives light from any height, any position.

Put handy-man talents to work to make a divider between beds for the time when you have two guests. When it's not in use, it stores at the end of the beds, against the wall. You might substitute a folding card table for the board.

You'll get lots of use from little space with a shelf arrangement such as this. Portable television set rests on a folding stool-table, has its own convenient chair. Set goes elsewhere when table is wanted as a luggage rack.

Chapter thirteen

Decorating ideas for halls and stairways

The first impression guests receive of you and your home is given by your entrance hall. It should reflect the same tastes and interests shown by decorating in the rest of the house. But since it's often darker than other rooms, and you pass through instead of living in it, a hall can usually take the gayer, brighter colors better than other areas. Other decorating ideas for halls and entrances:

1. A mirror for last-minute make-up and hat adjustments is a great convenience, particularly if the coat closet is also in the entrance hall.
2. A place to set mail, purses, gloves, will be useful. It can be a narrow shelf, or a chest that stores other items, too.
3. A chair or stool to sit on while putting on boots or rubbers will make you and your guests more comfortable.
4. In a narrow hall, shallow pieces of furniture will facilitate traffic.
5. Decorative handrails protect stairway walls. Or use plastic wall covering or paint that's washable.
6. When you buy stair carpet, tuck an extra yard under bottom riser. Shift a few inches occasionally to distribute wear.

Plan hall and stairway lighting for both beauty and comfort

You won't be working in the hall or on the stairway—except to clean—so soft, indirect lighting is usually the best choice.

In this entrance hall, a decorative fixture at doorway says "welcome," sheds a glow on the foot of the stairs. It is supplemented by a recessed ceiling fixture in the dark area leading to the room beyond.

If your home has no separate entry, it's possible to create one. Perhaps furniture arrangement or a screen will define the necessary area. Or, you might consider using carpet on the living room floor, with a blending color of hard-surface flooring in hall area. It's practical, too, since tracks can be wiped up easily.

Use your ingenuity to make sparkling, personalized accessories for the hallway

The handsome hanging scale is not an antique at all, makes a delightful substitute for the ordinary fruit bowl. It's an inexpensive brass scoop purchased from a restaurant supply house for under $10.

A pair of brass chains is brought around under the scoop and caught with swing hooks, as shown in the sketch at right. Then the unit is hung from a ceiling or wall bracket.

The marble dove perched so lightly on the fruit is actually floating on a strand of invisible wire that holds it firm—an ingenious way to steady a heavy breakable object.

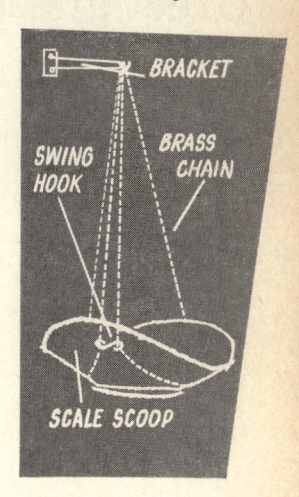

Elegance depends on decorating skill rather than on the money you spend

This formal entrance takes its decorating cue from the classic black and white tile arrangement, the Empire lines of the bench. Strong Napoleonic green of bench cover is emphasized by the impressive foliage arrangement, tones of pictures. You could copy dado with grass cloth, wallpaper border.

Greet guests with something of beauty

The mural on the wall of this entry was painted by its artist-owner. If you're no artist, you could achieve a similar effect with one of today's imaginative wallpaper murals, lending perspective in small space.

Old brass bird cage hung from overhead light troughs and filled with foliage is in the living room, but visible from hall, and subtly relates itself to the mural design.

A hanging wall shelf takes little space but adds much to a hall's attractiveness

If your entryway is small, use the walls to expand the decorating possibilities.

Narrow shelf suspended from the wall by brass chains gives space for a handsome display of fruit and flower arrangements.

Wall-mounted wood carvings above the shelf add handcrafted touch of color and hint of the owner's travels and tastes.

Louvered shutter doors that fold back upon themselves replaced conventional closet door that would have needed floor space in which to swing open.

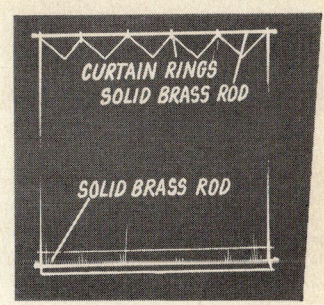

Drapery fabric stretched on rods attached to wall suggests entrance where there's no separate hall

The illusion of an entrance is created here with a fabric panel on the wall opposite to the front door, cut to the same width as a hall might be. It meets the guest's eye first as he enters the home.

This wall hanging is a panel of drapery fabric that's lined and stretched tautly between two heavy brass rods. See the diagram above for the details.

Idea borrowed from the Orient inspired this ornament

Oriental wind chimes are an imaginative yet inexpensive and easy-to-make decoration for a hall.

Tubes of bamboo of varying lengths are strung on linen cord. The finished bells are hung from ceiling hooks by fine wires so they will sway in the draft of air which each opening of the front door produces, gently chiming a welcome to your guests.

To make bamboo wind bells, decide where you want holes and center punch stock to accept drill tip so that it won't "creep" when drill starts.

Run cord in and out through the verticals, bottom of horizontal. Thread wires through top of horizontal to hang parallel; tie at top.

For entrance halls, try new ideas, new colors, new worksaving surfaces

Wood paneled upper walls with vinyl fabric dado make a heavy-traffic entrance hall simple to maintain, attractive, too. If you apply it yourself, the price of vinyl fabric is about 30 cents a square foot.

To get a similar effect at lower cost, paint the lower half and apply wood-patterned wall covering above. Papers patterned to resemble wood grain come in many styles, some protectively coated to make them washable, durable.

Floor-to-ceiling room divider forms an entrance hall

A screen made of traverse rod cord stretched tautly between floor and ceiling gives the feeling of a separate entrance hall even though the outer door opens into the living room.

An insert of hard surface floor covering inside the front door helps further the illusion of separation and is a practical solution to muddy feet problems. Abstract pattern was fashioned from leftover tile, and includes hues from over-all color scheme.

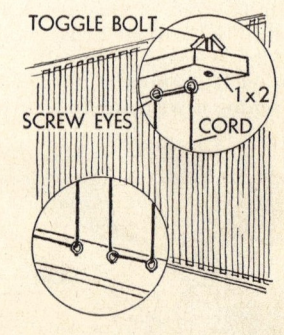

To make this room divider you'll need two 1x2s which are the length of the divider you wish to install.

Next, decide on the spacing of the cords and fasten screw eyes to both of the boards at the intervals you prefer.

Fasten one board to the ceiling, the other to the floor. Last step is to string cord through the screw eyes.

For a happy surprise, paper in Roman stripes lines a coat closet

Walls of pristine white that increase a hall's apparent dimensions, brilliant yellow floor and black and white furnishings give this foyer character and sophistication.

Inspired extra is the bright striped vinyl wallpaper which lines the coat closet.

If there's enough space and light, a foliage plant is always a pleasant decoration.

Gleaming metal and glossy foliage supply good textural contrast to an interior wall of brick

Interior brick walls, featured in many Contemporary homes, have their own interest of pattern and texture. But their appeal is sharpened when a contrast is introduced.

In this entrance area, shiny butterflies of pierced brass and green foliage plants offer variations of both texture and form with brick.

The covered wicker basket, decorative in itself, might be put to use as a hiding place for overshoes.

Tile flooring is appropriate to the functional simplicity of the over-all decorating style, is easy to maintain.

A light and cheerful look

Borrow an Oriental motif

Harmonious in a Contemporary home are horizontal lines of the low furniture, vertical contrast of picture or wall hanging.

Softening the contrast are the bare branches held in a brightly striped metal container.

→

Wash the walls with color

Bright gold like captured sunshine will keep this entrance cheerful on the dullest of days.

Gold of the coin-dotted wallpaper is exactly matched in the drapery fabric and in upholstery covering of the love seat.

Wall covering gives airiness

Graceful, leafy design of this mural wall covering follows the lines of the entrance hall staircase.

The delicacy of pattern creates a feeling of lightness that's to be desired in restricted areas that are lacking in adequate natural light.

should be your goal in decorating a hall

Establish traffic lanes, then arrange furniture accordingly

Some older homes have entrance halls large enough to accommodate a gracious furniture grouping.

With an arrangement like this, remember to keep the traffic lanes open that lead from the front door to the stairway and to other rooms.

Well-decorated entry has eye appeal, is convenient, and suits your needs

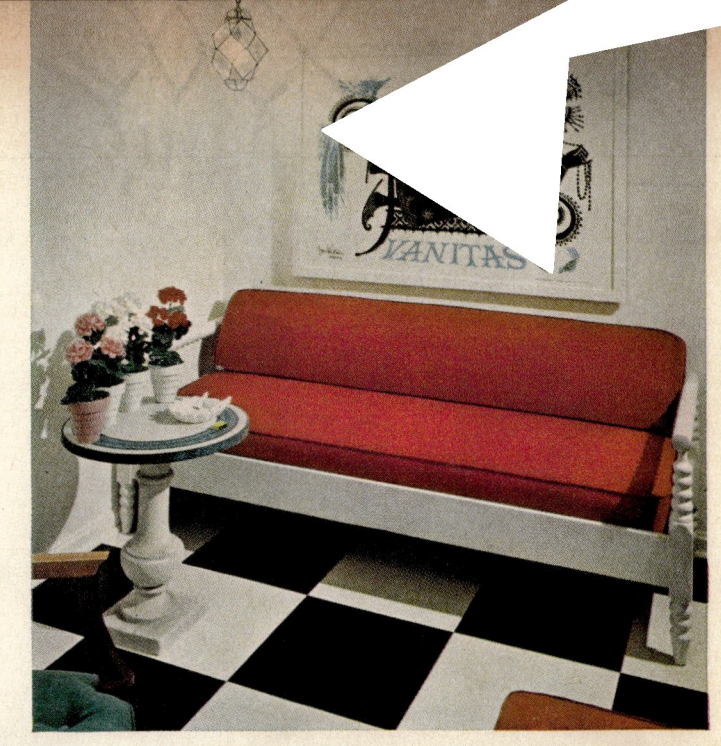

Guests are greeted by a striking yet inexpensively decorated entrance hall in this home.

An old-fashioned daybed has been painted white, given a new back bolster and dramatized with brilliant red velveteen upholstery.

←

Portable wall units or permanent extension of walls can form an entrance hall to suit your needs

Entrance hall is formed by extending the interior wall with two built-in units of the same walnut-faced plywood. Units also provide extra storage space and help channel traffic.

Concealed fluorescent trough-lights on top of partial wall are striking at night and accentuate the openness and vaulted ceiling of house.

The way you arrange furniture can set up an entrance hallway

Table and chair grouping lessens the feeling of walking right into living room by defining a traffic lane.

This is another way to create the illusion of an entrance hall when the front door opens into living room.

A furniture grouping on wall opposite front door ends perpendicular to line formed by table, chair grouping.

Search the attic for discarded furniture that can be turned into useful, decorative items

Often your entryway has room for only one piece of furniture so it's a good idea to make it an interesting, useful one.

An old sewing cabinet makes a novel as well as handy hallway chest. Six dollars worth of paint, varnish, and new hardware dressed it up to look like a new piece of furniture.

Side compartments were cut down to top of the second drawers and lined with sheet metal to make planters.

Wood cutting board is the basis for the unusual wall plaque. Three dollars supplied the keys, lock, and hooks. Discarded lamp needed fresh gilt and shade.

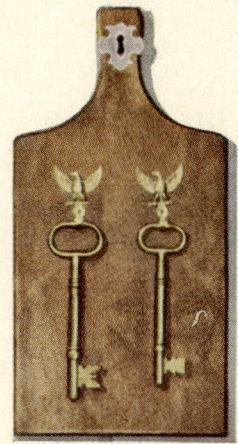

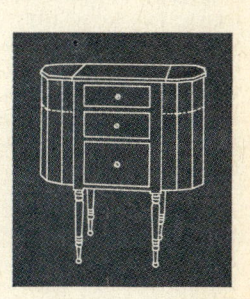

Entrance hall makes lasting impression on guests so take time and care in decorating it

A home planned for carefree living starts with the entrance hall.

Save work by choosing floor covering that's easy to care for. If the entry is small, keep the furniture close to the wall so traffic lanes stay clear.

If there is room, it's nice to have a table or chest for hats and purses and a place to sit down in comfort while you are putting on your rubbers or overshoes.

Take time to decorate your guest closet too. If there is no mirror in the hall put one on inside of closet door.

The first look and last look a guest has of your home is your entrance hall, so apply the same basic principles of decorating here that you do in all your rooms.

Credits and acknowledgments

Decorators

Adler, James (Affiliate, A.I.D.), p. 51
Altman's, p. 31
Anderson, Bob, p. 47
Armandroff, Jay, p. 144
Barrows, Ron, p. 46
Behrens, Ellen, A.I.D., p. 59
Bernard, Frederick H. Jr., A.I.D., p. 18
Bethune (A.I.D.) and Moore, p. 100
Bogart, Mel, p. 152
Brown, Everett, A.I.D., pp. 45, 58, 108
Catterton, Blair, A.I.D., p. 141
Chase, Nancy, N.S.I.D., p. 56
Chatfield, Harbine, A.I.D., N.S.I.D., p. 35
Clark, Duvie, p. 101
Clements, of Associated Decorators, p. 70
Cronley, Robert, A.I.D., pp. 21, 50, 70, 76, 153
Curtin, Bert, Interiors, p. 60
Day, Charles, A.I.D., p. 111
Decorative Manner, p. 150
de Grohe, Andre, N.S.I.D., of Englander Furniture Shops, p. 113
Dewey, Louise C., pp. 46, 93
Dietz, Marilyn, p. 65
Ellgren & Kamins, p. 40
Elrod, Arthur, A.I.D., pp. 12-13
Englander Furniture Shops, pp. 113, 155
Farmer, Walter, A.I.D., p. 94
Flemister, George, A.I.D., p. 50
Frampton, Tony, A.I.D., p. 78
Francis, Harry, A.I.D., p. 146
Fruit, Kenneth, A.I.D., p. 49
Fulkerson, Blanche, A.I.D., p. 151
Goode, Virginia, p. 107
Hanley, Robert, A.I.D., pp. 53, 77
Harbaugh, John, p. 82
Heuer, Marion, A.I.D., p. 155
Hoover, Fred, p. 48
Hudson, J. L., Co., p. 26
Kahane, Melanie, A.I.D., p. 53
Knoll, Roberta, p. 54
Lasseter, J. Haygood, A.I.D., p. 88
Lubliner & Himmel, pp. 43, 50, 88
Lynch, Joseph, of Gene Schneider, Inc., p. 135
Macaulay, James, p. 50
MacMorris, John W., A.I.D., pp. 36-37
Malka, Helen, p. 61
Mann, Aline, A.I.D., p. 115
Marshall Field and Co., pp. 64, 147
Mason, Betty, p. 129
Mercer, Kitty, of Dayton's Studios, pp. 50, 56
Miller, Richard, p. 46
Morin, J. Marshall, A.I.D., p. 41
Pagoria, Sarah, pp. 55, 74, 84, 85, 98, 106, 114
Peabody, Lawrence, A.I.D., p. 72
Perkins, John Astin, A.I.D., p. 40
Potter, John Joseph, p. 49
Roth, Louis Stark, p. 22
Salsbury, Allen Vance, A.I.D., pp. 79, 136
Sargent, Richard, p. 157
Shaw, Louis de Haven, A.I.D., p. 159
Simon, Sydney, A.I.D., p. 55
Smith, Elsie, A.I.D., p. 39
Smith, Elsie, A.I.D., and Dorothy Paul, A.I.D., p. 89
Smith, James M., A.I.D., and James W. Wills, A.I.D., p. 109
Sorkin, Sam, A.I.D., p. 19
Sporleder, Geraldine, A.I.D., pp. 24, 142
Stephenson, C. Eugene, A.I.D., pp. 43, 69
Stix, Baer & Fuller, p. 119
Tratt, Robert D., p. 145
Tumelson, J. Russell, pp. 54, 134
Weir, Maurice, A.I.D., N.S.I.D., p. 124
West, Beatrice, A.I.D., for Nat'l Homes Corp., pp. 148-149
Wilson, Jessica, A.I.D., pp. 60, 135

Photographers

Alderman's Studio, pp. 57, 58, 116, 117, 119, 122-123, 126, 127, 128
Bickel, John, p. 92
Bourdon, p. 96
Burgess, Guy, pp. 41, 100, 146
Cleveland, pp. 12-13, 39
Dant, pp. 93, 94, 95, 101, 159
de Gennaro, pp. 47, 48, 53, 64, 77, 85, 159
Gorski, p. 107
Harris, p. 132
Hedrich-Blessing, pp. 18, 19, 22, 28, 29, 30, 35, 43, 51, 54, 55, 59, 63, 64, 65, 66, 70, 72, 76, 79, 81, 82, 83, 88, 89, 92, 102, 105, 106, 111, 114, 115, 117, 133, 135, 136, 141, 143, 144, 145, 146, 150, 153, 156, 157
Hedrich, Bill, pp. 32, 33, 60, 89, 94, 106, 109, 115, 152, 158
Hedrich-Blessing, Suter, pp. 49, 50, 74, 75, 84, 85, 98, 104, 114, 121, 129, 147, 148-149
Hopkins, pp. 6, 7, 8, 9, 10, 11, 34, 51, 67, 97, 110, 116, 121, 132, 133, 136, 137, 138, 139, 151
Howland, pp. 31, 43, 56, 72, 95, 108
Hulin, Don, of Alderman's Studio, pp. 14, 15, 16, 17, 71
Lisanti, Inc., pp. 50, 66, 67, 69, 91, 118
Meisel, pp. 36-37, 96, 151
Rada, Rudi, p. 109
Reynolds, Photography, Inc., pp. 40, 49, 50, 78, 88, 103, 105, 135, 137, 139
Rogers, pp. 24, 40, 41, 142
Shirk, pp. 26, 54, 117, 134
Szanik, pp. 47, 89
Van Nes, pp. 53, 124
Weymouth, pp. 45, 46, 50, 58, 93, 108

Designers

Copp, Joseph Jr., p. 125
Doehr, Dale, p. 66
Jensen, Thomas H., p. 92
Jones & Duncan, pp. 28-29
Lucille Knoche Associates, p. 114
Lucille Knoche, I.D.I., p. 115
Lethemon, Howard C. Jr., p. 117
Thomas, Vivian, p. 85

Drawings by

Bielefeld Studios, p. 42
Howard, Ric, pp. 23, 84, 103, 118, 154, 156
Miller, Roy, p. 115
Richardson, Harry, pp. 20, 27, 30-31
Wells, Bill, pp. 62, 80, 120, 130
Whitaker-Guernsey, pp. 112-113, 118